# Mad, Bad, Dangerous to Know

*The Fathers of Wilde, Yeats and Joyce*

# Mad, Bad, Dangerous to Know

## The Fathers of Wilde, Yeats and Joyce

### COLM TÓIBÍN

**VIKING**
*an imprint of*
**PENGUIN BOOKS**

VIKING

UK | USA | Canada | Ireland | Australia
India | New Zealand | South Africa

Viking is part of the Penguin Random House group of companies
whose addresses can be found at global.penguinrandomhouse.com.

First published 2018
001

The acknowledgements on page 177 constitute an extension of this copyright page

Image on page 24 reproduced courtesy of the National Library of Ireland [EP WILD-WI (2) II];
photograph of John Butler Yeats by Alice Boughton on page 78 courtesy of the Library of Congress,
LC-DIG-ds-00785; image on page 134 courtesy of the Poetry Collection of the University Libraries,
University at Buffalo, The State University of New York

Set in 11/13 pt Dante MT Std
Typeset by Jouve (UK), Milton Keynes
Printed and bound in Great Britain by Clays Ltd, Elcograf S.p.A.

A CIP catalogue record for this book is available from the British Library

ISBN: 978-0-241-35441-4

www.greenpenguin.co.uk

For Mary-Kay Wilmers

Versions of three of these chapters were first given as the Richard Ellmann Lectures in Modern Literature at Emory University in Atlanta, Georgia in November 2017.

# Introduction

There is a peculiar intensity about some streets in Dublin that gets more layered the longer you live in the city and the more stray memories and associations you build up. With time, thoughts thicken and become richer, connect more. Sometimes this aura in the city can be greatly added to by history and by books.

On a busy day, nonetheless, it is possible to go into the General Post Office on O'Connell Street to post a letter or buy a TV licence and not think at all at first about the 1916 Rebellion, which used the Post Office as its headquarters, or about MacDonagh and MacBride, Connolly and Pearse, the men who led the Rebellion, or about Yeats's lines:

> When Pearse summoned Cuchulain to his side,
> What stalked through the Post Office? What intellect,
> What calculation, number, measurement, replied?

But then I turn and see the statue of Cuchulain, the mythical Irish warrior, made by Oliver Sheppard, which stands in the Post Office, and remember that Samuel Beckett once asked his friend Con Leventhal to betake himself 'to the Dublin Post Office and measure the height from the ground to Cuchulain's arse', because Neary in Beckett's novel *Murphy* wished to engage with the arse of the bronze Cuchulain by banging his head against it. Thus the mind, pondering on nothing much or the malady of the quotidian, can become bothered by heroes, by history, by head-bangers.

Before they closed the Bank of Ireland branch at the corner of Pearse Street and Lombard Street East, which is a continuation of

Westland Row, I used to walk down there regularly, since it was the branch where I had my account. Some days as I passed the National Library in Kildare Street on my way, I could think for a second about Leopold Bloom and the *Kilkenny People* and Stephen Dedalus and the ghost of Hamlet's father. I had studied in the National Library almost every weekday for two years between 1973 and 1975 so I could muse on who stole my yellow bicycle in the spring of 1975, and then wonder if they still make a Bulgarian wine called Gamza that Buswells Hotel across the road used to serve very cheaply by the glass in those years, or remember how a friend one day, while we both stood smoking outside the portals of the Library – the same portals that Joyce uses in *A Portrait of the Artist as a Young Man* – looking at the Dáil car park, remarked that Brian Lenihan, then a prominent politician, had hair that seemed to have been actually, by some ancient process, corrugated. Or recall, on my return from Spain in 1978, how strange I thought it was that there was only one real coffee machine in the whole city, in the Coffee Inn on South Anne Street.

And then I turn in to South Leinster Street, where the bomb went off in 1974, and I try to remember how many precisely it killed and wonder why there is no memorial there, and then try to remember what the bomb had sounded like as I sat in the Reading Room of the National Library that late Friday afternoon. It was like nothing much in fact; it was more the silence afterwards and the much more exact memory I have of the rest of that evening in the mad, panicking city, watching each parked car with a mixture of suspicion and fear and disbelief, then drinking in Toners pub in Baggot Street until the early hours, cello music playing on the radio, broken by a hush as each news bulletin came on.

And then I half-notice the sign on the gable end of the building on the opposite side of the street as the curve of Lincoln Place comes into view. It says Finn's Hotel. It is funny that the sign hasn't faded more. James Joyce got two books out of it, or the title of the second anyway. Finn. Finnegan. It was here on 10 June 1904 that Joyce met Nora Barnacle, who worked in the hotel. The two young strangers who had locked eyes stopped to talk, and they arranged to meet four days later outside the house where Sir William Wilde and his wife, Speranza, had lived, where they raised their son Oscar, who was four years dead by the time Joyce met Nora.

When Nora stood Joyce up on 14 June, Joyce wrote to her ardently, pleading for another date: 'I may be blind. I looked for a long time at a head of reddish-brown hair and decided it was not yours. I went home quite dejected. I would like to make an appointment but it might not suit you. I hope you will be kind enough to make one with me – if you have not forgotten me.' Later that day he wrote again: 'I hear nothing but your voice . . . I wish I felt your head on my shoulder.' They walked out together for the first time on 16 June, which is when their story began, and when *Ulysses* is set. It was lucky, I suppose, that their date wasn't in the middle of November, then it would have been a shorter book. Or on Good Friday, when the pubs used to be closed. The thought occurs to me for a moment, as I think of those closed pubs and wine sales off bounds on Good Friday, that it was a dry business, a crucifixion. Especially towards the end. Only water came out of the wound in his side.

\*

The street between Nora's hotel and Wilde's house is called Clare Street. Samuel Beckett's father ran his quantity surveying business from Number 6 but there is no plaque here. When their father died in 1933, Samuel Beckett's brother took over the business while Beckett himself, who was idling at the time, took the attic room. Like all idlers, he made many promises; in this case, both to himself and to his mother. He promised himself that he would write and he promised his mother that he would give language lessons. But he did nothing much. It would look good on a plaque: 'This is where Samuel Beckett did nothing much.'

Like Wilde and Yeats, Beckett belonged to that group of Protestant geniuses who thought that they should write down their thoughts just as their landowning and powerful and money-owning colleagues were clearing out of Ireland or learning to keep quiet. They all came from different rungs of the social ladder. At the top was Lady Gregory, who had a big house and plenty of tenants; and then John Millington Synge, who had a small private income, as Beckett and Wilde did, and a memory of glory; and then W. B. Yeats, who worked hard all his life; and also poor Bram Stoker and George Bernard Shaw. And then Sean O'Casey, who was nearly blind he was so poor. All of them baptized into the wholly unroman and highly protestant church. And none of them believed a word of it, except poor Lady Gregory, who did indeed hope for heaven, unless O'Casey's communism, which was of the high church sort – he supported the crushing of the Budapest Uprising in 1956, for example – was a sort of religion. It must be fun not believing in anything, and having your fellow countrypeople wanting you to clear off to England because of the very religion you don't believe in.

This must be why a few of them became interested in posing and twisting things around and developing their eloquence and working on their silence. It must be why Oscar Wilde loved finding an accepted set of truths and then turning them sharply inside out, and why George Bernard Shaw loved a paradox, and Elizabeth Bowen, who left later, loved the Irish Sea.

I turn into Westland Row, passing by Sweny's Chemist, and then down towards the bank. Mr Beamish, my old bank manager, retired now, gave me money when no one else would. Samuel Beckett too had a friend called Beamish, Noelle Beamish, an Irish woman who lived in the same French village as him during the war and left her long, utilitarian drawers out to dry beside her younger lover's little frilly underthings.

So much has disappeared; so much stays in the memory. The

bank is gone, the building is used for something else, and so, too, the old Academy Cinema, which was once the Antient Concert Rooms, where Joyce sang and where he set his story 'A Mother'. I saw Fellini's *Amarcord* in the Academy in the spring of 1975 with my friend Gerry McNamara. In those years, the Irish Film Censor used to cut the dirty scenes from films with a scissors, so it was only years later that I got to see the episode where the Italian boys all masturbate. It was not deemed fit for us then.

Gerry is more than twenty years dead now, and my friend Anthony Cronin, who introduced me to that bank and warned me not to push my luck if Mr Beamish gave me a loan, is over two years gone. He lived for some time around the corner from here in Magennis Place when he came back from London in the late 1980s with the writer Anne Haverty, whom he later married. He loved these streets and sidestreets, relishing corners. One of his early poems is called 'Liking Corners', and it praises the places

> Where corners collect the dust as well as sun –
> Warm brick, warm fingered stone and bits of glass,
> Minute particulars all afternoon . . .

In the years when he lived here, he wrote a love poem to Anne called 'Happiness' about making his way home along Westland Row. The poem opens:

> Sometimes, walking along Westland Row
> Thinking that Anna will be there before him,
> His happiness is so great,
> He is like a walking jar,
> Full to the very brim.

I miss his scepticism, his independence of mind, how funny he was. Once, after a play with much movement, little plot and no interval, a production much admired by all, he told me that it had permanently darkened his mind. 'Permanently?' I asked him. 'Are you sure?' He insisted that he was more than sure, he was certain: the damage had been permanent. And then a glimmer of slow amusement appeared in his eyes at the fact that at least we were out of the theatre now, away from all the terrible choreography and actors running around the stage. 'Oh when I realized there would be no interval,' he chuckled, 'I knew then that the damage would be permanent. That play has permanently darkened my mind.' He shook his head in mock despair.

When I was growing up in a small town two hours south of here, the same town where Anthony Cronin grew up, the train from Rosslare stopped at Westland Row as well as at Amiens Street on the north side of the city. So this street was my introduction to Dublin. I don't know what age I must have been, but young enough to believe that you must, in order to cross a street, look left and then right and then left again, only to be told by my father as he started crossing Westland Row that in Dublin that rule didn't really obtain, that if a car was far enough away then you could, in fact, cross quickly, even if it was moving towards you.

Westland Row was also a commuter stop for those going to work in the city centre from the south side of Dublin. These included the poet Thomas Kinsella, who worked in the Department of Finance on Merrion Street. His poem 'Westland Row', from his volume *Nightwalker*, published in 1968, captures that sense of coming down into the street from the station platform above:

> We came to the outer light down a ramp in the dark
> Through eddying cold gusts and grit, our ears
> Stopped with noise.

Kinsella noted the old diesel train passing along the rackety bridge overhead:

The engine departing hammered slowly overhead.
Dust blowing under the bridge, we stooped slightly
With briefcases and books and entered the wind.

Years ago, it must have been 1973 or 1974, when I sent Kinsella some poems I had written, he wrote me a long letter in response. I remember some of the words, although the letter is lost: 'Live whatever way you can or have to, and pay attention perhaps to American poetry as a way of noting what others are doing.'

Almost forty years later, when they were making a television documentary about Thomas Kinsella, I went with him and stood at the gates of a house outside the town where I am from. This was the house where his wife, Eleanor, was born – I remember her mother as a most engaging and skilful whist player. This was the house where Kinsella set his poem 'Another September', the title poem of his 1958 volume, and we stayed watching the 'apple trees, / Ripe pear trees, brambles, windfall-sweetened soil' that he had invoked more than half a century earlier.

As I move up Westland Row, reversing direction, going towards Clare Street, something in the air thickens. Much of the street is dingy-looking; some of it is even derelict. It could be a city street in a run-down quarter of anywhere in these islands – Glasgow, Liverpool, Newcastle, London. The buildings – most of them built in the 1770s – are mainly three stories over a basement. The ones on the right-hand side belong now to Trinity College. I know that Joyce's father spent time here, as did the parents of Oscar Wilde, John Stanislaus Joyce coming here in the 1870s, the Wildes two decades before that. It is hard not to imagine how desolate it must have been then in the years after the Famine when Dublin was a capital city from which the glory had departed. It had no parliament then, since Ireland had been ruled directly from Westminster following the Act of Union of 1800. As Belfast was becoming an industrial city, Dublin stagnated, or seemed to.

In his book *Modern Ireland*, Roy Foster wrote:

The non-industrial base of Dublin was one of the main reasons for the precarious and extremely impoverished condition of its proletariat by the late nineteenth century . . . The centre of the city was a byword for spectacularly destitute living conditions, exacerbated by the increasingly sharp division between the spacious bourgeois suburbs to the south and the central concentration of slum dwellings . . .

In the epilogue to his book *Dublin 1660–1860*, Maurice Craig began:

It is difficult to write with patience of the nineteenth century in Ireland. It is an era of slow decay and fitful growth . . . in truth the era has little discernible shape . . . For all its mass movements, it is an era of individuals, of occurrences apparently isolated and apparently without meaning . . . The capital has begun to take on an air of mild melancholy: after sixty years the loss of political status is beginning to induce an unmistakable feeling of provincialism . . . The personality of mid-Victorian Dublin is mysterious to our eyes: so much, we know, is stirring there: so little of it was apparent, or so it seems to us.

In his book *Dublin: The Making of a Capital City*, David Dickson, however, noted a growth in the lower middle class in the city that

came about for several reasons, but principally because of structural changes in the city economy from the 1830s, with the shift of manufacturing employment to commerce, and the re-emergence of Dublin as unchallenged national centre of wholesale trade . . . One-eighth of the male workforce by 1881 [the year before James Joyce was born; the year the Yeats family returned from London to Dublin and remained for six years] held transport-related jobs. Retail employment, large and small, was at least as important.

In 1862, the authorities created a new cattle market, which was, Dickson wrote, 'supposedly the largest such market in Europe . . . and meant that the North Circular Road became the corridor for the hundreds of fattened bullocks and sheep that were driven down to the cattle boats every day in late summer and autumn'. Dickson also charts the expansion of clerical employment in the city 'in every decade from the 1830s – in education and the police, in the prisons, hospitals and welfare institutions, in both civic and central government – with Dublin really benefiting from the high level of administrative centralization in Ireland compared with Victorian Britain'.

The nineteenth century was also a period of church-building in the city. Dickson notes that St Andrew's Church in Westland Row, where Leopold Bloom spends time in *Ulysses*, 'accommodated a standing congregation of 3,200'. The suburban train line that led south from Westland Row, the one from which Thomas Kinsella alighted, was the first to be built in the country. It was created two years before London's first suburban railway. Regular service began towards the end of 1834. It carried the people from what Roy Foster calls 'the spacious bourgeois suburbs to the south' into the city centre.

Dublin, then, was poor, down at heel, in the years when Oscar Wilde's father and W. B. Yeats's father and James Joyce's father lived in the city. Such growth as came was not due to industry or manufacturing; it came in the guise of transport and the increase in the number of clerks. Despite suburban expansion and improvement in infrastructure, the image of Dublin in the second half of the nineteenth century and the early years of the twentieth as a place of isolated individuals, its aura shapeless in some way, a place hidden from itself, mysterious and melancholy, remained intact, enough for James Joyce himself to see the city as 'a centre of paralysis', and for his younger brother, Stanislaus, who left Dublin in 1905 and did not return, to deplore in his book

*My Brother's Keeper* the lack of that sense of tradition that had nourished the work of many novelists elsewhere and allowed characters in fiction to face choices and chances and seek their destiny with a kind of equilibrium.

'In [James Joyce's] *A Portrait of the Artist,*' Stanislaus wrote:

> Dedalus speaks of a certain disadvantage at which Irish writers find themselves in using the English language. The very slight differences in the shades of meaning which English words may have for Englishmen can give pause, I fancy, only to Irishmen like Yeats or my brother, whose sensibility to words applies extreme tests. To me it seems that the real disadvantage of Irishmen is of quite a different nature. In Ireland, a country which has seen revolutions in every generation, there is properly speaking no national tradition. Nothing is stable in the country; nothing is stable in the minds of the people. When the Irish artist begins to write, he has to create his moral world from chaos by himself, for himself. Yet, though this is an enormous disadvantage for a host of writers of good average talent, it proves to be an enormous advantage for men of original genius, such as Shaw, Yeats, or my brother.

What is strange, as I move up this street in the scarce winter light, is how empty Westland Row might seem if you did not look properly, how ordinary and plain. Brick houses, the railway, one pub, a small supermarket, the Royal Irish Academy of Music, a church that is now too big and unwieldy, like a draughty old box, a few derelict buildings, even the buildings owned by Trinity College appearing sullen and withdrawn. Those images of Westland Row from the poems by Cronin and Kinsella could come to us as though created by mere lone voices, isolated sensibilities, solitary figures walking home or to work in a time that had remained what Maurice Craig called 'an era of individuals', a time when there was still, in Stanislaus Joyce's words, 'no national tradition', when every writer had to invent a world as though from the very beginning.

Among these individuals who began to animate the city in the nineteenth century, as Maurice Craig points out, was the figure of Sir William Wilde, who, when he married Jane Elgee, lived first in this street. His son Oscar was born in 1854 at Number 21 Westland Row on the right-hand side as I move away from Pearse Street going south. There is a small plaque in Oscar's honour on the building.

The Wildes moved around the corner to Number 1 Merrion Square soon after Oscar was born. Twenty years later, John Stanislaus Joyce moved his offices to Number 13 Westland Row. He and his mother may even have lived in this building, or in a nearby hotel. In their biography of Joyce's father, John Wyse Jackson and Peter Costello wrote of Westland Row: 'Though it is not usually seen as a Joycean district, this street seems to have retained its special significance for James Joyce.' Just as Joyce was to use Chapelizod, where his father first lived when he came from Cork to Dublin, in *Finnegans Wake*, there is, as Wyse Jackson and Costello made clear, an intensity in the way Westland Row is invoked in *Ulysses*, as though Joyce were evoking and exploring the spirit of his father's early life in Dublin.

Westland Row appears in Episode 5 of *Ulysses*, or Leopold Bloom appears in the street in that episode. It is ten o'clock in the morning on 16 June 1904 as Bloom walks away from the quays via Lombard Street East, passing Nichols the undertakers, which is still in business to this day. He stops to look in the window of the Belfast and Oriental Tea Company at 6 Westland Row, now gone. Then he goes into the post office at 49–50 Westland Row, also disappeared. Using the name Henry Flower, he asks if there are any letters for him, to find that there is a letter from Martha Clifford, who has answered an advertisement he has placed in *The Irish Times*. ('Wanted smart lady typist to aid gentleman in literary work.')

In Westland Row he bumps into an acquaintance called M'Coy, who has appeared earlier as 'secretary to the City Coroner' in Joyce's story 'Grace'. M'Coy has been drinking in Conway's at Numbers 31–2 Westland Row, now called Kennedy's; they talk about the death of Paddy Dignam and the news that Molly Bloom is going to sing in Belfast. In passing, they mention the names of several other characters from the stories in *Dubliners* – Hoppy Holohan, Bob Doran and Bantam Lyons – thus thickening the plot. (M'Coy's wife, who is a singer, also appears in *Dubliners*.) For a second, as he moves away, Bloom thinks about his father, who killed himself. Then he leaves Westland Row, moving to a smaller parallel street so that he can read the letter. Under the arch of the railway, having read the words of Martha Clifford, he tears up the letter.

He notes that 'An incoming train clanked heavily above his head, coach after coach' before he enters St Andrew's Church – which he calls All Hallows – by the back door, where he studies people receiving communion and makes one of the best jokes in the book when he considers the use of wine in the mass: 'Wine. Makes it more aristocratic than for example if he drank what they are used to Guinness's porter or some temperance beverage Wheatley's Dublin hop bitters or Cantrell and Cochrane's ginger ale (aromatic).'

Bloom, having mused further on the mysteries of religion, walks out the front door of the church, thus finding himself on Westland Row itself once more. He remembers that he must go to Sweny's Chemist at the top of the street, which up to recently was a normally functioning pharmacy but is now a sort of Joycean museum, where he has a lotion made up for Molly and where he buys a bar of lemon soap. In the shop, he is accosted by Bantam Lyons, who reminds him that the Ascot Gold Cup is being run that day. The race will be won by a horse called Throwaway, coming in at twenty to one. Since Bloom twice tells Lyons that he can keep his newspaper since he was going to 'throw it away' in any case, Lyons presumes that this is a tip for Throwaway. Later in the novel it will be presumed that Bloom, who is unaware of the name of the horse, has won money on the race.

Bloom then walks from Westland Row into Lincoln Place, passing by the back gates of Trinity College, and moves into South Leinster Street, where he will visit the Turkish Baths. 'Enjoy a bath now: clean trough of water, cool enamel, the gentle tepid stream. This is my body.'

Because the novel is set in 1904, Oscar Wilde and W. B. Yeats are already famous, as are Wilde's parents. Thus James Joyce as he moves his characters in these streets is circling the world of the two other writers. In Episode 10, one of his characters will halt 'at the corner of Wilde's house' at 1 Merrion Square. Later, one of the nationalist songs written by Lady Wilde will be invoked.

Oscar Wilde himself is a constant presence in *Ulysses*. In Episode 1, for example, when they discuss the mirror, they refer directly to Wilde's novel *The Picture of Dorian Gray*, published in 1891. In the same episode, Buck Mulligan says: 'We have grown out of Wilde and paradoxes.' In Episode 3, there is a reference to 'Wilde's love that dare not speak its name' and to his poem *Requiescat*, written in memory of his younger sister. In Episode 9, as they discuss Shakespeare, there is a mention of 'the Platonic dialogues Wilde wrote' and Wilde's 'Portrait of Mr W. H.'

W. B. Yeats and his two sisters also wander through the pages of Joyce's book as a source of considerable amusement to the author, it seems, and some of his characters. In Episode 1, Lily and Lollie Yeats appear as 'the weird sisters' who print books in Dundrum, and they will be referred to later as 'two designing females'. They had returned to Dublin a couple of years before *Ulysses* is set to establish the Dun Emer Press, which produced limited editions. (Wyse Jackson and Costello report an encounter between James Joyce and one of the Yeats sisters in 1903 or early 1904: 'She noted his "tennis shoes" and marvelled how the young man had told her that "he thought drink would soon end his father and then he would give his six little sisters to Archbishop Walsh to make nuns of".')

*Ulysses* also mocks W. B. Yeats himself. His statement on Lady Gregory's translation of the Táin: 'I think this book is the best that has come out of Ireland in my time,' is the cause of much mirth in the book. The novel also makes fun of the phrase 'strangers in the house' from Yeats's play *Cathleen ni Houlihan*. There is a parody of Yeats's poem 'Baile and Aillinn', published the previous year. In his broadside 'The Holy Office', written before his departure from Dublin in 1904, Joyce also mocked Yeats.

Yeats's grandparents and his father knew Oscar Wilde's parents and were part of the same small Dublin world. It would be fascinating to imagine that Joyce's father, when he moved into Westland Row with his mother, might have passed the Wildes on the street since their house was just around the corner, but he missed them by a few years. What connects Oscar Wilde with James Joyce, however, besides Wilde's presence in *Ulysses*, is that both writers knew W. B. Yeats, who supported each of them in times of difficulty.

Yeats in his *Autobiographies* wrote an account of a Christmas dinner in the late 1880s that Wilde invited him to, believing him to be alone in London:

> He had just renounced his velveteen, and even those cuffs turned backward over the sleeves, and had begun to dress very carefully in the fashion of the moment. He lived in a little house in Chelsea . . . I remember vaguely a white drawing-room with Whistler etchings, 'let in' to white panels, and a dining room all white, chairs, walls, mantelpiece, carpet, except for a diamond-shaped piece of red cloth in the middle of the table under a terra-cotta statuette, and I think a red-shaded lamp hanging from the ceiling to a little above the statuette . . . and I remember thinking that the perfect harmony of his life there, with his beautiful wife and his two young children, suggested some deliberate artistic composition . . . One

form of success had gone: he was no more the lion of the season and he had not yet discovered his gift for writing comedy, yet I think I knew him at the happiest moment of his life.

On the day before Wilde's trial began in May 1895, Yeats, who was almost thirty years old, called to Wilde's mother's house in London to express his solidarity with the author and deliver letters of sympathy that he had collected.

Twenty years later, when James Joyce was broke and wanted a pension from the British government, Yeats, who had known him first as an arrogant young writer in Dublin, wrote letters in his support, including one to Edmund Gosse, who had wondered, on behalf of the committee, if James Joyce actually supported the British cause in the First World War. Yeats loftily replied:

*My dear Ghosse [sic]: I thank you very much for what you have done; but it never occurred to me that it was necessary to express sympathy 'frank' or other wise with the 'cause of the allies'. I should have thought myself waisting [sic] the time of the committee. I certainly wish them victory, & as I have never known Joyce to argue with his neighbours I feel that his residence in Austria has probably made his sympathy as frank as you could wish. I never asked him about it in any of the few notes I have sent him. He had never anything to do with Irish politics, extreme or otherwise, & I think disliked politics. He always seemed to me to have only literary & philosophic sympathies. To such men the Irish atmosphere brings isolation, not anti English feeling. He is probably trying at this moment to become absorbed in some piece of work till the evil hour is passed. I again thank you for what you have done for this man of genius.*

As I walk past the Wildes' house on Merrion Square, I note that W. B. Yeats lived on the Square too in the years after his marriage, and his brother had a studio on Fitzwilliam Square close by. In the National Gallery, also on Merrion Square, there is work by Yeats's father and his brother, Jack, and also his two sisters.

Slowly, courtesy of the marriage between William Wilde and Jane Elgee in 1851 and the marriage between John B. Yeats and Susan Pollexfen in 1863 and the marriage between John Stanislaus Joyce and May Murray in 1880, a set of networks and webs of association began to evolve in the city, intensifying the narrative and making it more mysterious, offering the atmosphere in Dublin a hidden and powerful undertow in the years before the 1916 Rebellion that politics did not offer, nor commerce either.

This newness in the city exalted the idea of isolation, individuality, aloneness. It remained an era of individuals, with writers and painters creating their moral worlds from chaos by themselves, for themselves. Leopold Bloom moves alone in the city, as Stephen Dedalus does. Wilde in his London world stood alone too, as he suffered alone. And Yeats stayed proudly aloof, as Joyce did in his exile. Ireland offered them isolation, as Yeats wrote to Gosse. It was a sort of gift.

Their fathers, too, stood apart, following no route that any community had charted. They lived as though there were no guidance, no map; there was only waywardness and will, hard frenetic work in the case of Sir William Wilde and wit and indolence in the case of John B. Yeats and John Stanislaus Joyce. They created chaos, all three of these fathers, while their sons made work. The sons became expert finishers – of plays, poems, novels, essays, and indeed their own fragile selves. In their own likeness, they made the world we walk in.

Just as Wilde would invoke his father in one passage of *De Profundis* and Joyce commemorate his father in his fiction, Yeats in a late poem called 'Beautiful Lofty Things' remembered his father at the Abbey Theatre in the wake of the riots protesting against Synge's *The Playboy of the Western World*:

My father upon the Abbey stage, before him a raging crowd:
'This Land of Saints,' and then as the applause died out,
'Of plaster Saints'; his beautiful mischievous head thrown back.

All three writers lived in a city that did not have a rich theatrical tradition or a great publishing industry – David Dickson notes
that in 1871 'nearly all the fiction sold in Dublin, whatever its
genre, was now produced in London'. They had fathers whose
energy could be mined and used, just as they themselves offered
an energy that any walker in the city can mine and use. They
reimagined the ordinary, run-down streets, left traces and glowing clues that transform Westland Row and the streets around it
as I walk back from the bank.

There is a beautiful essay that captures how much this matters
by the poet Eavan Boland, who was a student at Trinity College
in the 1960s. It is called 'Becoming an Irish Poet'. It begins: 'When
I was a student I could choose which way to go home.' She could
leave Trinity by the front gate or slip out into Clare Street and
then go into Merrion Square:

> Merrion Square is one of those old treasures of Georgian Dublin.
> An ambiguous gift of colony. On the nights I walked down to it, it
> was eerie and silent. But a century earlier it would have been dif-
> ferent. The whole neighbourhood was then the centre of Dublin
> professional life. I could easily summon it as I stood there in the
> dark. Haloed gaslight. Fashionable carriages over the cobbles. The
> rush and noise of a ruling class.

Boland remembers a house on a corner: 'One façade pointed
at the trees of the square. Another looked towards Trinity. It was
a tall structure, not quite rid – even in the present moment – of
the hubris of its origins. But I was not looking up because of a
bygone era. I was there for a previous tenant.'

That tenant was the poet and translator Jane Elgee, also known as Speranza, the wife of Sir William Wilde, the mother of Oscar Wilde. Boland seeks to imagine her 'in the tumultuous decade of the 1840s . . . She was writing poetry and trying to have it published. She had not yet read her legendary son's comment: "Others write the poetry that they dare not realize." For her, there would be no distance between poetry and self-realization.'

Boland muses on Speranza's finding a nation through her poems and wonders about this, and also about the poems themselves, which she finds unconvincing. But that is not why she is standing here outside the Wildes' house. She remains fascinated that the woman who wrote these poems was so certain of her loyalties:

> On those cold nights, I still believed origin was simple and grasp-able. I was still convinced, after my own nomadic childhood, that coming to a cause and place which seemed to embody both was a rich source for a poet. And so when I looked up at Speranza's window, it was not her failures I was imagining. It was her happiness.

The next paragraph begins: 'It would take me years to see my mistake. To understand the difference between the place a poet claims and the place a poem renders.' Boland would in her own work not merely claim the suburbs of Dundrum, but allow her poems to render the interior life in the houses there so that the space took on an aura that was fully inhabited, courtesy of the poems' cadences.

I am standing at the very place where Boland stood, looking at the plaque to Sir William Wilde, unveiled in 1971. The plaque reads: 'Sir William Robert Wills Wilde, 1815–1876, aural and ophthalmic surgeon, archaeologist, ethnologist, antiquarian, biographer, statistician, naturalist, topographer, historian, folklorist, lived in this house from 1855 to 1876.' The unveiling, attended by the daughter-in-law of Oscar Wilde, with thirty to forty people present and speeches in Irish, attracted the attention of the Irish police, who moved in to note down the names of the speakers, believing that they had to be from some illegal organization. It took some time to convince the cops that the crowd was there merely to commemorate a great man and that those marking the occasion included the founder director of the Irish Central Statistics Office, the President of the Royal College of Surgeons in Ireland, and a past President of the Royal Irish Academy.

Across the street, just within the railings of Merrion Square, there's a funny, colourful statue of Oscar Wilde, the pose languid enough to attract the attention of even the most enlightened group of police.

To get to the memorials to W. B. Yeats and to James Joyce, two writers who spent their lives working on the differences and connections between the places they claimed and what the work they made rendered, I will have to walk along Clare Street, pass the Mont Clare Hotel, where my parents spent their honeymoon – my father, who had been a student in Dublin, my mother later complained, showed her too many churches – and cross over to where Greene's Bookshop once was; there used to be a little post office at the back of it – and walk along South Leinster Street – Beckett and his father used to enjoy the same Turkish Baths as Leopold Bloom – again and turn into Kildare Street, where in Joyce's story 'Two Gallants', not far from the porch of the Kildare Street Club, 'a harpist stood in the roadway, playing to a little ring of listeners. He plucked at the wires heedlessly, glancing quickly from time to time at the face of each new-comer and from time to time, wearily also, at the sky.'

I walk past the National Library, where Yeats's papers are, and some Joyce manuscripts. The Library opened in 1890, having been built by the firm owned by Samuel Beckett's grandfather. Yeats used the Reading Room, as did Joyce. Yeats, as Roy Foster wrote, later 'remembered his youthful self sitting in the National Library in Kildare Street "looking with scorn at those bowed heads and busy eyes, or in futile revery listening to my own mind as if to the sounds in a sea shell . . . I was arrogant, indolent, excitable."'

In December 1898, Yeats wrote to Lady Gregory from the Library: 'My only time of leisure is when I come here where I am now writing & go to a table away among the private passages of the National Library. The librarian lets me go & read where I like & so I escape drafts & noise.' Joyce would set Episode 9 of *Ulysses* in the Library. This is where Stephen has his long debate about *Hamlet* and Shakespeare. In this building, 'Coffined thoughts around me, in mummycases, embalmed in spice of words.' At the end of the chapter Buck Mulligan will spot Leopold Bloom leaving the building and whisper to Stephen: 'The wandering jew . . . Did you see his eye? He looked upon you to lust after you. I fear thee, ancient mariner. O, Kinch, thou art in peril. Get thee a breechpad.'

The domed Reading Room has not changed since the time of Yeats and Joyce. It has the same light and layout, the same noises, perhaps even some of the same people, or maybe they just look similar. And the same sounds: whispered consultations with the librarians; chairs being pushed back; the seagull cries on the outside reminding us how close the sea is and the port; some coughing; and then a sudden pounding silence as heads are bowed low in the holy sacrament of reading.

These days you have to get a reader's ticket to use the National Library. In the 1970s when I came here every day, no one checked your credentials: they presumed that you were doing serious research and treated you accordingly.

You signed your name in the big old book as soon as you went into the Reading Room. You found a table, making sure that the light worked, and you went about ordering your books for the day, using the old catalogues that were like ledgers. I don't think that I have ever been as happy as during those first months in the National Library as I read what I could find about the Dublin book trade in the reign of Charles II. I looked around me a lot and I regularly went out for a smoke. In those days the College of Art was sandwiched between the National Library and the Dáil (you could hear the bells calling the members of parliament to come and vote). The art students were as exotic and colourful as jungle birds. They were either very tall or very small; they had either very long hair or very short hair; some of the boys looked like girls and vice versa. We, the readers in the National Library, compared to them, were a dull-looking lot dressed in faded tweeds. The art students, on the other hand, seemed to have made their own clothes, or bought them second-hand. They were perfect in every way.

I walk now towards St Stephen's Green by the side of the Shelbourne Hotel. This, as Roy Foster wrote, was Yeats territory: 'the heart of their city was not the plebeian landmark of Nelson's Pillar (hub of the tramway system) but Stephen's Green'. John B. Yeats had his studio here in the years when he finally returned to Dublin before he went to New York. It is in St Stephen's Green itself, within its railings, in an area hidden by shrubbery with an entrance that is not obvious to the eye, that Henry Moore's monument to W. B. Yeats is situated. This circle where the bronze stands, in its strange isolation, its purity, its odd nobility, is one of the most beautiful and powerful places in Dublin, full of a secret energy worthy of the great old ghost.

The statue of Joyce's head faces Newman House, the site of the Catholic University, opened in 1854 with John Henry Newman as rector until 1858. In 1880, it became University College Dublin. James Joyce studied here from 1898 to 1902. Now his face in bronze stares placidly towards the railings. In *A Portrait of the Artist as a Young Man*, he has Stephen Dedalus call Stephen's Green 'my Green'. The poet Gerard Manley Hopkins came to live and teach in Newman House in 1884 and died here in 1889. He wrote his dark sonnets in an upper room in Newman House where he woke and felt 'the fell of dark, not day'. There is a plaque outside now to Newman, Hopkins and Joyce. When *Ulysses* appeared, a professor who taught at Trinity College said: 'James Joyce is a living argument in favour of my contention that it was a mistake to establish a separate university for the aborigines of this island – for the corner boys who spit into the Liffey.'

I have news for this professor: we spit no more. We write books now and make software. We travel home peacefully to the suburbs when the day is done.

I walk out of the green by the Leeson Street exit and cross into Lower Leeson Street. I am going home. The books are waiting, as are the empty pages. Soon I will start writing the story of the three prodigal fathers. I have walked enough. Some city streets, in the wake of these figures and their sons, are haunted.

*An Eminent Victorian:*
*Sir William Wilde*

W Wilde

The prisoner, an Irish poet and playwright, would later die in his early forties, his reputation blighted by scandal and by allegations of egotism. In a book, he would describe Reading Gaol, where he was incarcerated, as 'a handsome building, erected in red brick after the manner of an old castle, with battlements and towers'.

What surprised him was the abundance of flowers growing in the exercise yard:

It was an amazing sight. There were not merely flowers, a sight astonishing enough in itself; there was a prodigality of flowers. Then some of us remembered the cause. One of the graves unlocked the secret. It was marked with the letters C. T .W., and the date, 1896, to whom Oscar Wilde's 'Ballad of Reading Jail' had been inscribed, and in celebration of whose passing the poem had been penned.

In his book he quoted from Wilde's poem:

> But neither milk-white rose nor red
> May bloom in prison air;
> The shard, the pebble, and the flint,
> Are what they give us there:
> For flowers have been known to heal
> A common man's despair.
>
> So never will wine-red rose or white,
> Petal by petal, fall
> On that stretch of mud and sand that lies

> By the hideous prison-wall,
> To tell the men who tramp the yard
> That God's Son died for all.

'So Wilde had sung,' the prisoner wrote, 'not in protest, but in bitter acceptance . . . But for us who came after him with the memory of his song in our minds, the miracle had been wrought . . . for the great yard was a lake of leaf and bloom . . .'

The prisoner who came after Wilde and quoted from his poem was Darrell Figgis, one of a group that had been involved in the 1916 Rebellion in Ireland. Many of them had been held first in other British prisons but now were transferred to Reading where, together in the small women's section of the prison, they were allowed to associate freely. They had been selected by the British authorities because they were believed, often wrongly, to be the leaders or the main troublemakers among the Irish nationalists. They included Arthur Griffith, the founder of Sinn Féin, and Sean T. O'Kelly, later President of Ireland. Despite their reputation, they were, while prisoners, quiet and peaceful, easier to manage than the Irish political prisoners who would be incarcerated in Reading two years later.

Many of this first batch of Irish prisoners in Reading wrote poetry, enough indeed for one of them, Ernest Blythe, who was later managing director of the Abbey Theatre for more than quarter of a century, to complain about this in rhymes of his own:

> To Reading Gaol I have been sent
> And must endure the punishment
> That every bloke is writing rhyme
> And I must praise it every time.

Darrell Figgis and the other prisoners who served time at Reading after the Rebellion were released in December 1916. A hundred years later, in 2016, three years after the prison, which had been used in recent years as a place for younger offenders, was closed, I went there in the spring and walked around its empty corridors and bare cells. By this time, the section where the Irish political prisoners had been held had been demolished, but the main prison was as it had been when it was built in 1844, each floor a cruciform shape, which meant that each of the four corridors could be seen from a single, central vantage point.

That day, there was no hint of the ghosts of the Irish political prisoners, and no hint either of the presence of Oscar Wilde. Instead, it was filled with the atmosphere left by the young offenders, cell after cell with metal bunk beds riveted into the wall, a small table and two stools, a metal sink closer to the window that was high in the wall opposite the door, and then a toilet on the other side of a partition. There was a sense of bleakness and desolation about each cell. The idea of what it might be like to be cooped up here all day and night with another person was fully palpable.

Outside in the world there were young men walking the streets who had suffered the boredom, the tedium of these confined spaces just three years before.

The only moment that day when I felt that I could imagine the prison as Oscar Wilde might have experienced it was when we were in the basement close to the exercise yard and the man who was in charge of the building casually mentioned that this room that led to the yard was where prisoners were flogged. I remembered this passage from Wilde's letter to the *Daily Chronicle* shortly after his release:

> About three months ago I noticed amongst the prisoners who took exercise with me a young man who seemed to me to be silly or half-witted . . . On Saturday week last I was in my cell at about one o'clock occupied in cleaning and polishing the tins I had been using for dinner. Suddenly I was startled by the prison silence being broken by the most

horrible and revolting shrieks, or rather howls, for at first I thought some animal like a bull or a cow was being unskilfully slaughtered outside the prison walls. I soon realized, however, that the howls proceeded from the basement of the prison, and I knew that some wretched man was being flogged ... Suddenly it dawned upon me that they might be flogging this unfortunate lunatic ... The next day Sunday 16th, I saw the poor fellow at exercise, his weak, ugly, wretched face bloated by tears and hysteria almost beyond recognition ... There, in the beautiful sunlight, walked this poor creature – made once in the image of God – grinning like an ape, and making with his hands the most fantastic gestures, as though he was playing in the air on some invisible stringed instrument ... All the while hysterical tears, without which none of us ever saw him, were making solid runnels on his white swollen face ... He was a living grotesque.

For a second as I walked around the bare exercise yard, I could almost imagine Wilde confined here under this sky, and what he saw that day, and the sounds he had heard earlier when he was in his cell.

Later in the year, on Sunday 16 October 2016, I returned to Reading Gaol, which was now open to the public courtesy of Artangel, an organization that promotes the showing of art or the making of art in odd and unexpected places. Some of the cells had artworks on display by artists including Vija Celmins and Marlene Dumas. And over the previous weeks there had been readings by actors and others from Oscar Wilde's *De Profundis*.

I had agreed to be locked in Wilde's cell, the cell known as C.3.3, on the third floor of Block C, for the entire afternoon of that Sunday to read an almost complete version of *De Profundis*, which would take five and a half hours. It would be streamed on to a screen in the prison chapel; visitors could also come and look into the cell through a peephole in the door, although I could not speak to them, nor they to me. All I could do was read

Wilde's text in the very space where it was written, written in a time when prisoners were held in solitary confinement, when they were forced to maintain silence even in the short spell each day when they circled the exercise yard.

*De Profundis*, a 55-000-word letter addressed to Lord Alfred Douglas, written by Wilde during the final months of his sentence, is a strange literary creation, a hybrid text. It was the only work that Wilde produced while serving his two-year sentence. On 2 April 1897 the prison governor informed the Prison Commission that each sheet of the manuscript 'was carefully numbered before being issued [to Wilde in his cell] and withdrawn each evening', but it is more likely that Wilde was given greater freedom to revise and correct the pages. The governor was informed by the Commission that the letter could not actually be sent, but instead should be kept and handed to the prisoner on his departure from the prison.

Wilde, when he was released, gave the manuscript to his friend Robert Ross, who had two copies made; one he sent to Lord Alfred Douglas, the other he later lodged in the British Museum. Sections from Ross's copy were published in 1905 and in 1908. Although it had many errors in transcription, a complete version, based on the original manuscript, was published in 1949.

*De Profundis* is a cross between an intimate address, filled with accusation and urgent statement, and a set of eloquent meditations on suffering and redemption and self-realization. It is a love letter and a howl from the depths. Its tone is hushed and wounded. It is written with passion, intensity and some wonderfully structured sentences. It is lofty, haughty, proud, and also humble, soft-toned, penitent. It was written in a range of different moods rather than composed by a stable imagination. It darts, shifts and often repeats itself. It was created for the world to read and composed for the eyes of one man and written to satisfy the prisoner himself, sometimes all at the same time. It is a great guilty soliloquy about love and treachery, about despair and darkness. It is also often wise and filled with sorrowful, eloquent, melancholy truth.

When I was alone in Wilde's cell that October Sunday with the pages in front of me, pages I had already read over and over in silence, I still had a problem. I did not know what sound the sentences Wilde had written in this solitude should make when read aloud. I did not know what the voice should be like when spoken to these cold four walls.

Theatrical? Angry? Passionate? Dramatic? Or quiet? Hushed? Whispering? Or should I try to find a real voice, a voice that urgently wanted to be believed or heard, or, maybe even more importantly, a voice in the wilderness seeking to re-establish its own sound so that the speaker's identity and sense of self, so crushed by solitude and prison rules, could find a space again, a clearing where the speaker could find comfort, even if no one actually attended to the words he spoke or wrote?

The letter was written by a prisoner to someone who was free, by an older man to a younger one, by a writer to an idler, by the son of a man who had earned his privilege to the son of a man who had inherited his. It was written in the tone of a letter that desperately needed to be written but might never be sent.

But it was also written by an Irishman to an Englishman. And it was that last idea that gave me a clue about how to start speaking the words that Wilde had written. I would begin by speaking them in my own voice. And I would speak as though I were talking to one person only, one person whose spirit was close at hand, and see as I went along if I would find out something new about the text that might have eluded me in all my silent readings of it.

What I noted as I read was not only the venom that came to the surface at any mention of Douglas's father, the Marquess of Queensberry, but also a sort of disdain Wilde felt for Queensberry, as though he were a figure from a lesser culture or indeed a lower species. The conflict in *De Profundis* was not only between the writer and the putative recipient, but also between Wilde's pride in his own class, his own family and his contempt for Douglas's father and indeed the entire world that produced him.

As a result of Wilde's imprisonment, 'your father', he wrote scathingly, 'will always live among the kind pure-minded parents of Sunday school literature'. Douglas's mother, he wrote, saw that 'heredity had burdened [Douglas] with a terrible legacy, and frankly admitted it, admitted it with terror: he is "the only one of my children who has inherited the fatal Douglas temperament"'. Being the son of the Marquess of Queensberry was, Wilde wrote, a kind of doom: 'Through your father you come of a race, marriage with whom is horrible, friendship fatal, and that lays violent hands either on its own life, or on the lives of others.' In *De Profundis*, Wilde also alluded to the general dislike of Queensberry by his own family when he recalled their offer to pay Wilde's costs if he brought a case against him, writing 'that [Douglas's] father had been an incubus to them all: that they had often discussed the possibility of getting him put into a lunatic asylum so as to keep him out of the way: that he was a daily source of annoyance and distress to your mother and to every one else'. But this was nothing to Douglas's personal, particular hatred for his father, which was, Wilde wrote, 'of such stature that it entirely outstripped, overthrew, and overshadowed your love of me. There was no struggle between them at all, or but little: of such dimensions was your hatred and of such monstrous growth.'

Later in the letter, he saw connections between father and son: 'Whenever there is hatred between two people there is bond or brotherhood of some kind. I suppose that, by some strange law of the antipathy of similars, you loathed each other, not because in so many points you were so different but because in some you were so like.'

Wilde resented being used as a pawn in the game between father and son and insisted 'that I had something better to do with my life than to have scenes with a man drunken, déclassé, and half-witted as he was'.

The word 'déclassé' is interesting here. In *De Profundis*, Oscar Wilde refers to Lord Alfred Douglas as 'a young man of my own social rank and position'. But this view, in a country acutely alert to differences in rank, would not have been widely shared. Wilde was merely the son of an Irish knight while Douglas came from two aristocratic families and had a title. While Wilde's father worked for a living, Douglas's father had inherited his wealth. In Douglas's world, Wilde was an outsider, an interloper.

In the message he left at Wilde's club, the message that would cause the famous libel action, the Marquess of Queensberry alleged that Oscar Wilde was 'posing as a somdomite', as he spelt it. He might have added that Wilde was also posing as someone who held a social rank and position higher than it really was. This, in the England of 1895, might have been seen by many as a rather more serious accusation.

Wilde came from a long tradition of Irishmen who had created themselves in London. He was an artist, he moved freely in society, often using an English accent. He had been to Oxford. He invented himself in England much as his parents had invented themselves in Dublin. In *De Profundis*, he suggested that his own wit and cleverness were not merely attributes, but were themselves a sort of social rank.

This idea of rank coming from words and wit had belonged to his parents too. In the absence of any other aristocracy in residence in Dublin, Sir William and Lady Wilde represented a type of grandeur that they had built with their books and their brains, their independence of mind and their high-toned eccentricity.

When Wilde described himself in *De Profundis* as 'a lord of language', he was suggesting then that this title is loftier by far than Lord Alfred Douglas's title.

In *De Profundis*, Wilde was alert to his own inheritance, to who his parents were and what they had achieved, as much as he was concerned to denigrate and undermine and insult the family of

Lord Alfred Douglas. He quotes Douglas's own disparagement of his mother's hospitality as 'the cold cheap wine of Salisbury'. Indeed, he presented Douglas's parents as quite tedious and vulgar, involved in some dreary and unnecessary and primitive dispute.

How he referred to his own parents is notably different. When he listed what he lost at the time of his bankruptcy, he included the 'beautifully bound editions of my father's and mother's works'. In passing, he referred to lines by Goethe, which his mother often quoted, 'written by Carlyle in a book he had given her years ago, and translated by him', as though it were the most natural and ordinary thing for Carlyle to give a book to his mother.

But the most significant passage about his parents comes when he wrote of his mother's death, which occurred while he was in prison: 'She and my father had bequeathed me a name they had made noble and honoured, not merely in literature, art, archaeology, and science but in the public history of my own country, in its evolution as a nation.'

Thus when he wrote the passage in *De Profundis* describing his own importance:

> I was a man who stood in symbolic relations to the art and culture of my age. I had realized this for myself at the very dawn of my manhood, and had forced my age to realize it afterwards. Few men hold such a position in their own lifetime, and have it so acknowledged . . . The gods had given me almost everything. I had genius, a distinguished name, high social position, brilliancy, intellectual daring . . .

he was echoing the tone he had used to describe his parents' achievements. He was not only establishing his own importance in the world, but in emphasizing that he had 'a distinguished name' and 'high social position', as opposed to the 'terrible legacy' of the Douglases, he was asserting his own parents' importance, and integrating his own achievement with theirs, an achievement that, he notes, included Ireland's evolution as a nation.

In the way he presented his parents in his letter to Douglas, Wilde was invoking a sense of his own evolving country as a place that could confer honours in a manner that was more authentic and meaningful than the neighbouring island.

Thus in his cell, as Wilde wrote his long letter, he was in no doubt about what he thought of Douglas's parents. He also managed to describe with hushed grief the memory of receiving the news that his mother had died:

> No one knew better than you how deeply I loved and honoured her. Her death was terrible to me . . . What I suffered then, and still suffer, is not for pen to write or paper to record. My wife, always kind and gentle to me, rather than I should hear the news from indifferent or alien lips, travelled, ill as she was, all the way from Genoa to England to break to me herself the tidings of so irreparable, so irredeemable, a loss.

As I go on reading the letter, I am interested in the silences that lurk between the words in *De Profundis*, the things that Wilde does not say, that he glosses over, that he seems almost to avoid. While Wilde had time to say everything he needed to say, there is one figure almost missing from the pages of his letter, a figure whose life has a considerable number of similarities with that of Wilde himself.

This figure is his father, more than twenty years dead when Wilde wrote *De Profundis*. Since Wilde put so much energy into letting it be known that he had invented himself, it is easy to understand how having a father might have seemed at certain moments quite unnecessary for him. Posing as a fully fledged orphan was another of his modes. And like Lord Bracknell in *The Importance of Being Earnest*, his father does not need to appear.

While Sir William's books and the name he bequeathed to his son are mentioned in *De Profundis*, there is no moment when Wilde's father is fully evoked, no moment when anything particular is said about who Sir William Wilde was, and what he did, nothing about how his own search for fame, his own notoriety, has strange echoes with events in the life of his son, nothing about how Oscar Wilde emerged not, like Jay Gatsby, from his Platonic conception of himself, but from a family, and that many of the ambiguities in his personality, many of his talents, came from his father.

William Wilde, the son of a doctor, was born in County Roscommon in Ireland in 1815. He studied medicine in Dublin where he became friends with Robert Graves, a doctor and painter nineteen years his senior. It was Graves who recommended him to a patient about to embark on a cruise of the Mediterranean in 1837. William Wilde's first book, entitled *Narrative of a Voyage to Madeira, Teneriffe, and along the Shores of the Mediterranean, including a visit to Algiers, Egypt, Palestine, Tyre, Rhodes, Telmessus, Cyprus, and Greece*, in two volumes, was an account of this journey.

This book set a tone that made clear how omnivorous William Wilde's interests were. As Terence de Vere White wrote in *The Parents of Oscar Wilde*:

> Everything interested him – the appearance of the people, their lives, the state of each place, its history, commerce, antiquities, girls, dress, public institutions . . . He was a census-maker born, but his interests were too wide and his imagination too vivid to be a mere statistician . . . Wilde had the eye of the scientific explorer. Very little escaped him.

In Egypt, Wilde was assailed by the local youth:

> The whole body of donkey boys, with their animals, rushed upon us with one accord, pushing, jostling and abusing each other in a

most unintelligible jargon; and a half a dozen laying hold of us at once attempted to place us, *nolens volens*, on their donkeys. I was literally lifted off and on three of them, before I could employ my stick to any advantage, to deter others from plucking me off the one on which I had at last secured a seat . . . The whole scene is really so ludicrous, that it is worth witnessing for once, after which I would advise all travellers to provide themselves with a good stout *koorbag*, which is made of the hide of the hippopotamus, and forms a staple article of commerce with the inhabitants of Upper Nubia, and on the Blue River; it is the only remedy for an Alexandrian ass-boy.

When Wilde writes about the excitement of walking through the narrow streets of Algiers, and when he offers descriptions of the sheer exotic nature of Algiers ('The day was the most exciting I had experienced since I left England. Nothing can exceed the variety and incongruity of costume, and the appearance of the people you meet with in the narrow streets of Algiers'), it is difficult not to think of the account his son would give of a stay in the city with Lord Alfred Douglas almost sixty years later, just months before his downfall, in a letter to Robert Ross from Algiers: 'There is a great deal of beauty here. The Kabyle boys are quite lovely. At first we had some difficulty procuring a proper civilized guide. But now it is all right and Bosie and I have taken to haschish [sic]: it is quite exquisite: three puffs of smoke and then peace and love.'

William Wilde had interests other than peace and love. His son's frivolity as revealed in his letters (and in the account of André Gide, who was with him and Douglas) was matched by the father's seriousness. While Oscar Wilde's interest in the local youth occupied him to the exclusion of much else, William was fascinated by monuments and the diverse ethnicities, by the religions and traditions he came across, by local politics, as well as by the wildlife.

On the ship he had a dolphin dragged on board and he dissected it over three days, thus gathering material for a scientific paper.

On his return to Dublin, William Wilde worked as a doctor, but also gave lectures on any subject that interested him, from anatomy to geology to archaeology to ethnology. He began to write for the *Dublin University Magazine*, whose editors included the lawyer and politician Isaac Butt, who became a regular dinner guest at Wilde's house in Westland Row, and the novelists Charles Lever and Sheridan Le Fanu. (His son Oscar would also contribute to the magazine in 1877, when, at the age of twenty-three, he wrote an account of the opening exhibition of the Grosvenor Gallery in London.)

William Wilde also travelled to London, where he delivered lectures about his travels to the British Association, which he had joined in 1839. He then proceeded to Vienna and Berlin to pursue his medical studies, visiting also Prague, Munich and Brussels, where he stayed with Charles Lever and visited the site of the Battle of Waterloo. In 1843 he published *Austria, Its Literary, Scientific and Medical Institutions*, and in 1849 a book on Jonathan Swift, *The Closing Years of Dean Swift's Life*.

Jane Elgee, whom William Wilde married in 1851, began to publish poetry in the Young Ireland journal *The Nation* in 1846 when she was twenty-five. *The Nation* was a radical, nationalist journal. Charles Gavan Duffy was one of the founders and the first editor. As Jane got to know the editors and contributors, she wrote to a friend: 'There is an earnestness almost amounting to fanaticism in the Patriotism of all the Young Ireland Party combined with great genius and a glowing poetic transcendentalism. They are all poets and I know of no genius outside their circle in Ireland.'

In 1848, while Charles Gavan Duffy was being held for sedition, Jane Elgee wrote editorials in *The Nation* under her pen name, Speranza. One began: 'The long pending war with England has actually commenced,' and included the line: 'O! for a hundred thousand muskets glimmering brightly in the light of Heaven.'

The charges against Gavan Duffy included the writing of this seditious editorial. In a protracted trial, he was represented by Isaac Butt, who refused to allow Elgee to appear to admit that it was she who had written it. In court, when Elgee tried to speak from the gallery and state that she was the culprit, she was silenced. Isaac Butt pointed out to the judge that the editorial could not, in fact, have been written by Charles Gavan Duffy, who was in prison at the time of its publication. According to newspaper reports:

> The Solicitor-General observed that it had been intimated to him that this article was written by a lady . . . [He] then said that he would not press the matter. He should be sorry the lady who wrote it should incur any risk by coming on the table; she was a lady of respectability and most respectably connected, and if she had been led into this folly [then] if the lady had been his sister or his daughter [he would not want to put her in the witness box].

The charges against Charles Gavan Duffy were dropped. In 1852 he was elected to the House of Commons, resigning his seat some years later to emigrate to Australia. Isaac Butt would feature subsequently in the life of William Wilde and his wife, and would also be a friend of John B. Yeats. His name would appear twice in *Ulysses* and once in *Finnegans Wake*, and the bridge over the Liffey named after him was invoked in *Ulysses*. He also, it seems, had a connection to Jane Elgee before her marriage. In a letter to his son in 1921, John B. Yeats wrote of Jane Wilde: 'When she was Miss Elgee, Mrs Butt found her with her husband when the circumstances were not doubtful, and told my mother about it.'

Butt was two years older than William Wilde. He studied at Trinity College Dublin, where Oscar Wilde would also be a student, and became a Professor of Political Economy there and a lawyer. A staunch conservative, he opposed Daniel O'Connell's campaign for the Repeal of the Act of Union between Great Britain and Ireland, but his experiences in the Great Irish Famine of 1845 to 1847 changed his politics, making him into a Federalist rather than a Unionist. His work defending various Irish revolutionaries, including the Young Ireland leaders and the leaders of the Fenian Rebellion of 1867, also softened his conservative views. He was a member of the British Parliament from 1852 to 1865 and from 1871 until his death in 1879. He was the first to use the phrase 'Home Rule' to describe the need for political separation between Ireland and Britain and was the leader of the political group in Westminster that supported Home Rule. His political influence waned over the last years of his life, as younger members, led by Charles Stewart Parnell, wishing to use more radical measures, took over the Irish Parliamentary Party. Besides his fame as a lawyer and a politician, Butt also enjoyed various romances, and was, on occasion, heckled at public meetings by the mothers of his illegitimate children.

As a young man, William Wilde also fathered a child, known as Henry Wilson, born in 1838. By the time of his marriage, he had also had two further illegitimate children, Emily and Mary, born in 1847 and 1849, who were taken care of as wards by William's eldest brother, Ralph. (John B. Yeats believed that the mother of these two girls kept a 'black oak shop' in Dublin.)

William Wilde, in the years before his marriage, was emerging not only as a famous doctor, specializing in diseases of the eye and ear, founding the first Eye and Ear Hospital in Dublin, but also as an important antiquarian, topographer, folklore collector and archaeologist in a time when the study of ancient Ireland was becoming both fashionable and politically resonant. On his return to Dublin from his voyage in the Mediterranean, he became friendly with George Petrie, twenty-five years his senior, who had done much to revitalize the antiquities committee of the Royal Irish Academy, and was responsible for its acquisition of important Irish manuscripts. Petrie painted in watercolour, made sketches, collected music and wrote extensively on archaeology and early Irish history.

William Wilde worked with Petrie in County Meath, north of Dublin, discovering the remnants of lake dwellings, known as crannógs, and recovering a large number of artifacts, which were put on display in the Royal Irish Academy. William delivered a paper to the Academy on the finding in Meath in 1839 and was soon elected as a member. He was twenty-four years old. He was part of a group that travelled to the Aran Islands, where they collected stories and songs and studied customs and manners.

In the preface to his book *The Beauties of the Boyne, and Its Tributary, the Blackwater*, published in 1849, William wrote:

> It may be regarded as a boast, but it is nevertheless incontrovertibly true, that the greatest amount of authentic Celtic history in the world, at present, is to be found in Ireland; nay more, we believe it cannot be gainsaid that no country in Europe, except the early kingdoms of Greece and Rome, possesses so much ancient written history as Ireland.

*The Beauties of the Boyne*, written shortly after the Great Irish Famine, is a detailed and meticulous guide book, but it is also a way of suggesting, in a time when the very name of Ireland carried a burden of poverty and misery, that the Irish landscape itself possessed grandeur and nobility, and that the archaeology of the Boyne Valley offered resistance to any idea that Ireland could be easily integrated either spiritually or politically with England.

While the parliaments of the two countries had merged in 1801, it was evident from Wilde's book that the essential spirit of Ireland stayed implacably apart. That spirit was held in graves and churches and towers, signs in the landscape of a rich and complex life fully intact many centuries before the English efforts to civilize the country, so to speak, began.

The tone of the narrative is engaging – 'of all the modern towns in Ireland, of our acquaintance, we know few to vie with Trim in dirt, laziness and apathy' – and filled with interesting speculation:

> It is very remarkable . . . how frequently we find some of the earliest Christian remains in the vicinity of pagan mounds, tumuli and other ancient structures, as if the feeling of veneration remained round the spot; and, though the grove of the Druid was replaced by the cashel of the Christian, still the place continued to be respected, and the followers of the early missionaries raised their churches and laid their bones in the localities hallowed by the dust or renowned by the prowess of their ancestors.

Wilde's observations on the difference between the treatment of pagan and Christian monuments remain fascinating as he wrote about the complexities surrounding respect and belief in the Ireland of his time: 'It is a fact, strange but true, that the peasant, who will not . . . for love or money, touch a stone, or remove a mound believed to be of pagan origin, will wantonly pollute, or, for ordinary building purposes, dilapidate the noblest monastic structure, or the most sacred Christian edifice.'

Wilde's Boyne Valley was a set of layers, a palimpsest of competing cultures. Near Navan, he found a decaying castle, 'marking the boundary of the English Pale: it tells of the worst days of misrule in this unhappy land, where, without conquering the proud hearts, or gaining the warm affections of the Irish, the Anglo-Norman barons, who, with mailed hearts as well as backs, neither civilized nor enriched the country, resided amongst us'.

It is clear from his book that Wilde is aware of the difficulties inherent in any effort to describe the Irish landscape with political neutrality. Any reader in the aftermath of the Famine would be alert to the contemporary implications of his comment on the decaying castle. Wilde, however, wanted it both ways. In his preface, he wrote like a true and loyal subject:

> Her Majesty Queen Victoria, with her illustrious consort, has just visited this portion of her dominions, and by their coming amongst us, have done more to put down disaffection, and elicit the loyal feelings and affections of the Irish people, than armies thousands strong, fierce general officers, trading politicians, newspaper writers, and the suspension of the Habeas Corpus Act etc, etc. Let us hope that her welcome visit will be soon repeated.

One wonders what Jane Elgee would have made of his views on the Queen and her illustrious consort. One possibility is that she would have understood completely the need for duplicity or at least careful ambiguity, or seen the unease within the text as natural, part of a dual inheritance. Also, in the aftermath of the trial of Gavan Duffy, the trial that refused to try her, she had become disillusioned and abandoned the direct seditious rhetoric apparent in the editorials she wrote.

This idea of unstable and gnarled allegiances, of some beliefs as a sort of veneer, was something that would become, in turn, an essential element in the life of Sir William Wilde himself and the lives of his wife and his son. It was their very instability and unpredictability from which they would get much of their notoriety and power. No one was ever sure what they believed in, where their loyalty lay. Their identities were fragile, wavering, open to suggestion, and open also to pressure.

William Wilde and Jane Elgee and, indeed, Isaac Butt were eminent Victorians in Ireland and lived in a time when Dublin had no parliament and when revolutionary fervour in Ireland was ill-fated, half-hearted or part of a literary rather than a serious political culture. They themselves were a strange, unruly ruling class in Ireland, not accepted as fully Irish and not wealthy landowners either. They, with much to say, lived in an in-between state. Until they made connections (William as an antiquarian, Jane as a poet and translator and Butt as a lawyer) with the Ireland of their time, they were oddly powerless. But once the connections were made, their power was considerable.

It depended, however, on the ambiguity of their position, on their ability to draw power from two opposite sides without having fully to obey a set of rules to which either of these two sides adhered.

To a large extent, they could do whatever they liked. William Wilde, for example, had no difficulty in accepting a knighthood for his work on the medical implications of the census returns, and his wife, despite her efforts to be arrested in 1848, was happy to be known as Lady Wilde, and indeed was often referred to in this way by Oscar.

Even though the Wildes were Protestants in a mostly Catholic country, with family origins in England and Scotland rather than Ireland, their loyalty was not only to a distant England, from which some of their power came, but also to a distant Ireland, a dream nation of traces and fragments, a country that might once more, with their assistance, materialize.

What is fascinating is how the duality of their position made its way into the sexual realm. The Wildes and Isaac Butt were an essential part of respectable Dublin society at the height of Victoria's rule, yet they flouted the rules of sexual morality. Wilde's illegitimate son, for example, was completely acknowledged by him and also became a doctor, working closely with his father, writing the first book in English on ophthalmoscopy.

The Wildes saw themselves as English or Anglo-Irish as it suited them. Wilde was Surgeon Oculist in Ireland to the Queen and he and his wife's sense of privilege and power derived from the very oppressor of the ancient culture that they both admired and studied. Their interest in this culture, however, gave them an edge, lifted them out of their own circumstances and gave them an astonishing individuality and independence of mind.

Their dual mandate allowed them to throw good parties and caused them to be noticed and to be remembered. Lady Wilde was prone to grandiloquence, telling a fellow poet: 'You, and other poets, are content to express only your little soul in poetry. I express the soul of a great nation. Nothing less would content me, who am the acknowledged voice in poetry of all the people of Ireland.' She saw herself in lofty terms: 'I should like to rage through life – this orthodox creeping is too tame for me – ah, this wild rebellious ambitious nature of mine. I wish I could satiate it with Empires, though a Saint Helena were the end.'

Many accounts were subsequently written of the Wildes. George Bernard Shaw remembered William Wilde 'dressed in snuffy brown; and as he had the sort of skin that never looks clean, he produced a dramatic effect beside Lady Wilde (in full fig) of being, like Frederick the Great, Beyond Soap and Water, as his Nietzschean son was beyond Good and Evil.' Harry Furniss wrote that

> Lady Wilde, had she been cleaned up and plainly and rationally dressed, would have made a remarkably fine model of the Grande Dame, but with all her paint and tinsel and tawdry tragedy-queen get-up she was a walking burlesque of motherhood. Her husband resembled a monkey, a miserable-looking little creature, who apparently unshorn and unkempt, looked as if he had been rolling in the dust . . . Opposite to their pretentious dwelling in Dublin were the Turkish Baths [the Baths where Leopold Bloom would go, and Samuel Beckett and his father] but to all appearances neither Sir William nor his wife walked across the street.

W. B. Yeats saw that any understanding of who Oscar Wilde became had to take into account the mixture of formidable intelligence and unmoored strangeness exuded by his parents. 'Of late years,' he wrote in *The Trembling of the Veil*, 'I have often explained Wilde to myself by his family history.' Yeats recounted an old Dublin riddle: ' "Why are Sir William Wilde's nails so black?" Answer: "Because he has scratched himself." '

> They were famous people [Yeats wrote] and there are many like stories; and even a horrible folk story . . . that tells how Sir William Wilde [as an eye surgeon] took out the eyes of some man . . . and laid them upon a plate, intending to replace them in a moment, and how the eyes were eaten by a cat . . . The Wilde family was clearly of the sort that fed the imagination of Charles Lever, dirty, untidy, daring . . . and very imaginative and learned.

Lady Wilde, Yeats wrote, 'longed always perhaps, though certainly amid much self-mockery, for some impossible splendour of character and circumstance . . . I think her son lived with no self-mockery at all an imaginary life; perpetually performed a play which was in all things the opposite of all that he had known in childhood and early youth . . .'

While these accounts were all written many years later – Shaw's in 1930, Furniss's in 1923, Yeats's in 1922 – and have to be read in the light of Oscar Wilde's disgrace and his mother's eccentric salon in London after her husband's death, there are contemporary accounts of the Wildes that note their willingness to be strange. Sir William Rowan Hamilton, for example, wrote to a friend about Jane Wilde in 1855 when Oscar was just one year old: 'She is undoubtedly a genius herself . . . She is almost amusingly fearless and original and *avows* (though in that as in other respects she perhaps exaggerates what is unusual about her) that she likes to make a *sensation*.'

Hamilton wrote her many letters, some oddly ardent, and took her seriously. Although they were easy to mock, the Wildes, like their son, also took themselves seriously. Other contemporary accounts of the Wildes show that they were much respected and admired and were indeed influential.

Sir William, as Terence de Vere White wrote, 'set himself against quackery and superstition in medicine. It is only necessary to glance at the advertisements in the newspapers of the day to see how much scope there was for reform.' Wilde's biographer T. G. Wilson takes the view that he was 'one of the two greatest English-speaking aurists of his time'. Wilde was appointed editor of the *Dublin Quarterly Journal of Medical Science*. He founded and ran St Mark's Hospital in Dublin, one of the leading ophthalmic hospitals in the British Isles. In 1853 he published the first significant textbook on aural surgery, *Practical Observations on Aural Surgery and the Nature of Treatment of Diseases of the Ear*, which was also published in America and in German translation. The following year he published *On the Physical, Moral, and Social Condition of the Deaf and Dumb*.

A medical procedure – an aural incision – was called after him, and he was credited with developing the first dressing forceps as well as an aural snare called Wilde's snare. He was the first to understand the importance of the middle ear in the genesis of aural infections.

Wilde and his wife continued to work on folklore and legend. The young Bram Stoker, when he was alone in Dublin in the early 1870s, gravitated to their house, where there was much talk of ghosts and superstitions. Sir William had published *Irish Popular Superstitions* in 1852; his wife published two volumes of Irish folklore and fairy lore. Roy Foster wrote of the influence of these books: 'Her folklore volumes profoundly influenced the young Yeats . . . they may also have been read by Bram Stoker . . . Both of them [the Wildes] were interested in Transylvanian legends, which may provide a possible link to *Dracula*.'

In the preface to her second book, Lady Wilde displayed an

eloquence that would have made Lady Bracknell proud: 'Thus to the primitive races of mankind the unseen world of mystery was a vital and vivid reality; the great over-soul of the visible, holding a mystic and psychic relation to humanity, and ruling it through the instrumentality of beings who had strange powers either for good or evil over human lives and actions.'

While William, in his work as a travel writer, historian, biographer and antiquarian, could reach what one writer called 'outlandish assumptions', he had, at the same time, or perhaps a moment later, a well-ordered mind and an ability to collect facts, classify and analyse information and write clearly and at times passionately about monuments, ruins and archaeology. He also made a significant contribution to Irish life in his work as a Census Commissioner.

William Wilde was, in fact, a distinguished statistician. In 1841 when the Census Commission needed to find out more about the causes of death in Ireland and were seeking a doctor with some fluency in Irish, an awareness of folk habits, a knowledge of the country and an enthusiasm for statistics, Wilde was the one chosen, even though he was only twenty-six. The fact that he was a member of the Royal Irish Academy and the British Association certainly helped, but it may also have mattered that he was a young doctor of modest means and would be likely to do the work.

Collecting information in Ireland was fraught with difficulty. People were suspicious of outsiders coming to investigate them. Thus, as Terence de Vere White wrote, 'the first census of Ireland, taken between the years 1813 and 1815, had been a failure. This was partly due to the not unnatural suspicion of the people that any government effort would work to their disadvantage . . .'

William Wilde's *Report upon the Tables of Deaths* in the 1841 census ran to 205 tables and 78 foolscap pages of closely written analysis, including a 94-item classification of diseases, using colloquial terms, Irish names and English translations, and then creating a standard system of description by which the diseases could be tabulated. For example, he noted the different terms for scrofula that were commonly used in Ireland: *'The Evil, King's Evil, The Running Evil, Running Sore, Felloon, Bone Evil, Glandular Disease, an Impostume; in Irish Easbaidh bragadh, deficiency in the neck; Fiolún, the treacherous disease; Cneadh Cnáithneach, the wasting ulcer; Cuit bragach, cuts in the neck.'* It is obvious from this that analysing medical census returns required nuanced linguistic knowledge and sensitivity to local lore as much as statistical skills.

In an essay on Wilde's demographic work, published in the *Irish Journal of Medical Science* in 2016, P. Frogatt wrote how Wilde

> examined the 1,187,347 deaths which the census had enumerated as having occurred since the previous (1831) census, and he looked for any associations between each death and the usual suspects— that is age, sex, occupation, poverty, fever, etc. He had to devise some ingenious methods of calculation of comparative estimates, e.g. he used medians instead of means, 'proportionate' mortality and other devices because he had no way of knowing how many births had taken place since 1831, and hence had no base line. Apart from everything else the whole exercise showed Wilde's grasp of statistical principles, unusual at the time, and his demoniacal energy, drive and ingenuity. The census exercise itself and its enthusiastic reception whetted Wilde's appetite for more, and he welcomed his appointment as 'The Assistant Commissioner' (no longer just a 'contracted official') for the forthcoming 1851 census.

Wilde was a Commissioner for the 1851, 1861 and 1871 censuses. In preparing the questions for the 1851 census in Ireland, his inclusion of some questions about physical and mental handicaps was unique and original. Such data had been gathered in no other country. Some of the information was compiled during the main census; other elements by supplementary enquiry. When the returns for 1851 came in, Wilde wrote two of the volumes, more than seven hundred pages, dealing with the information that the census yielded about disease and mortality. He also oversaw the work on the eight other volumes. Since death registration was not introduced in Ireland until 1864, Wilde's work on mortality was invaluable. And since the statistical work on the 1851 census dealt with mortality during the Great Irish Famine, the information he gathered is immensely important.

Also, because the evidence collected showed the obvious connection between poverty and mortality, Wilde's work was of considerable political significance and displayed independence of mind since he did not flinch from criticizing the government for its policies on health and social welfare in Ireland, basing his views on his exhaustive and energetic and accurate research. As one historian wrote: 'William Wilde saw the practice of scientific medicine as offering a means of deliverance from historical catastrophe for Irish society.'

In his statistical and epidemiological work, Sir William Wilde was at the very centre of the Victorian impulse in Ireland, which was to map the country, integrate it, make sense of its past and present. In matching the study of Ireland's realities and its heritage with systems of study in place elsewhere, as he did, Wilde was effectively undermining the very wildness and otherness of the country that he was at the same time busily charting. Wilde, filled with a mixture of idealism and patriotism and dutiful harmlessness, was part of a system that saw its function as modernizing, civilizing.

Wilde's high sociability and the hard work he put into so many different projects, some of which required clarity of mind and sharp focus and others of which needed raw enthusiasm and an ability to imagine and speculate, came at a cost or were signs indeed of a complex personality. Frogatt noted the sheer volume of work which Wilde personally got through with the help of admittedly quite a number of clerks, usually a dozen or so but at times up to 30 or more . . . while at the same time he was also busy conducting his professional medical and other rather more alluring affairs. The pace is caught in the tone of his letter to the Chief Secretary seeking his seemingly originally promised £1,800 fee though now he was being offered only £700 . . . 'I gave up all society and recreation for 18 months (November 1854–May 1856) and more than once impaired my health by the incessant daily and nightly labour devoted to this voluminous work.'

Wilde's enthusiasm for work and company, his general tirelessness, included a dark side that became apparent to his wife. In an undated letter, Jane wrote to a Scottish merchant and man of letters, John Hilson, whom she had befriended before her marriage, that although her husband was, as Emer O'Sullivan quotes in her book *The Fall of the House of Wilde*:

the best conversationalist in the metropolis, and author of many books, literary and scientific . . . he has a strange, nervous, hypochondriachal home nature that the world never sees . . . My husband so brilliant to the world envelops himself . . . in a black pall and is grave, stern, mournful and silent as the grave itself . . . when I ask him what could make him happy he answers death and yet the next hour if any excitement arouses him he will throw himself into the rush of life as if life were eternal here. His whole existence is one of unceasing mental activity . . .

A year after their marriage, the Wildes' first son, Willie, was born. Oscar was born two years later, in 1854, and their daughter, Isola, in 1857. The year before Oscar's birth, his father bought Illaunroe, a fishing lodge on Lough Fee in Connemara in the west of Ireland on thirteen acres of land. Later, he built another house ten miles away, at Moytura on Lough Corrib. The year after Oscar was born, the Wildes moved from their house in Westland Row to a much grander Georgian house at Number 1 Merrion Square, where they employed six servants.

The children were included in the atmosphere of sociability and intellectual enquiry to which their parents dedicated their lives. In 1880, Oscar wrote that 'at eight years old [he] heard every subject demolished at his father's dinner table, where were to be found not only brilliant geniuses of Ireland, but also the celebrities of Europe and America'.

In July 1857 the Swedish writer Lotten von Kræmer and her father, who was the governor of Uppsala, visited the Wildes. Although it was one o'clock, the butler let them know that Mrs Wilde was still in bed. When William Wilde appeared, von Kræmer noted that

> the noble figure is slightly bowed, less by years than by ceaseless work . . . and his movements have a haste about them which at once conveys the impression that his time is most precious . . . He carries a small boy in his arm and holds another by the hand. His eyes rest on them with content. They are soon sent away to play, whereupon he gives us his undivided attention.

At the time of the Kræmer visit, William Wilde was involved in cataloguing the holdings of the Royal Irish Academy, a project that had foundered on a number of occasions and that he had agreed to take on alone. As Emer O'Sullivan wrote: 'The catalogue was no mere inventory of objects. It provided a detailed description of every article, together with its history and provenance, demanding in turn a vast hinterland of numbered references, historical suggestions and quotations.'

The work was exhausting and beset with controversy as Wilde

decided to use drawings and wood engravings rather than photo-graphs and to catalogue by type rather than chronologically. In 1859, he wrote to the council of the Academy: 'Had I known the amount of physical and mental labour which I was to go through when I undertook the Catalogue, I would not have considered it just to myself to have done it; for I may fairly say, that it has been done at the risk of my life.'

The decision by the Academy to stop funding the project caused Wilde much distress. Lady Wilde wrote after his death: 'The necessary funds were, at last, collected to continue Parts II and III, Sir William contributing largely, with his usual liberality towards all national objects; but there the work stopped, whether from want of funds or want of interest among members of the Academy, it is difficult to say.'

While Part II of the catalogue was published in 1860, Part III in 1862, Part I was completed in time for a visit of the British Associ-ation for the Advancement of Science, which had a meeting in Dublin in August 1857. As Secretary of Foreign Correspondence to the Royal Irish Academy, William Wilde invited the Association's Ethnological Section to the Aran Islands. Seventy of the members were conveyed to the largest of the islands by a steam yacht char-tered in Galway. Wilde led the scholars through the island, jumping over walls and climbing hills, using a small whistle to assemble them.

On the evening of the second day, when they had sufficiently studied the ancient monuments, William Wilde organized a ban-quet for the visitors within the walls of the pagan fortress of Dun Aengus, the most spectacular site on the island, which forms a semicircle on the edge of a high cliff with a sheer drop of almost a hundred metres to the Atlantic below. Among them were the poet Samuel Ferguson and the painter Frederick Burton.

The writer Martin Haverty, who was also among the company, recalled: 'This was our culminating point of interest – the chief end and object of our pilgrimage . . . This was the Acropolis of

Aran . . . the venerable ruin which Dr Petrie described as "the most magnificent barbaric monument now extant in Europe".' Haverty described the unpacking of hampers, the sherry, the 'abundant' dinner. 'It was a glorious day,' he wrote, 'the sun being almost too warm, notwithstanding the ocean breeze which fanned us, and groups of the islanders looked on from crumbling ruins around.' There were many speeches made – by the Provost of Trinity College Dublin, by the French consul in French, by George Petrie, who proposed a toast to the local man who had been his host thirty-five years earlier when he was the first serious archaeologist to study the monuments of the island.

In his speech, William Wilde appealed to the islanders to protect the fort, which had suffered since Petrie's earlier visit:

> Remember, above all, that these were the works of your own kindred, long, long dead, that they tell a history of them which you should be proud of, that there is no other history of them than these walls, which are in your keeping. You have a great right to be proud of them; they are grand monuments of the brave men your forefathers were, and of how they laboured and how they fought to defend the land they left to you and your children. Do you defend them in peace as they defended them in war, and let your children's children see strangers coming to honour them, as we have done today.

Once the speeches were done, according to Haverty, 'a musician, with bagpipes, played some merry tunes, and the banquet of Dun Aengus terminated with an Irish jig, in which the French consul joined, *con amore*'.

Connecting with foreign scholars, as he did in Dublin and on the Aran Islands in 1857, was part of William Wilde's daily work. In the early 1860s he was made an honorary member of the Antiquarian Society of Berlin, and received a diploma from a Royal Society at

Uppsala and an honorary doctorate from Trinity College Dublin. The citation for his knighthood in 1864 read: 'Mr Wilde, I propose to confer upon you the honour of knighthood, not so much in recognition of your high professional reputation, which is European, and has been recognized by many countries in Europe, but to mark my sense of the services you have rendered to Statistical Science, especially in connection with the Irish Census.'

At the knighthood ceremony in Dublin Castle, Jane Wilde wore, according to one of the newspapers, 'a train and corsage of richest white satin, trimmed handsomely in scarlet velvet and gold cord, jupe, richest white satin with bouillonnes of tulle, satin ruches and a magnificent tunic of real Brussels lace lappets: ornaments, diamonds'. William's knighthood was, as Emer O'Sullivan emphasizes in her book, widely welcomed. The *Freeman's Journal*, for example, wrote:

> A more popular exercise of the vice-regal prerogative, nor one more acceptable to all classes in Ireland, could not possibly have been made, for no one of the medical profession had been more prominently before the public for the last twenty-five years in all useful and patriotic labours than Doctor (now Sir William) Wilde . . . the fact that he established, and has recently endowed, one of the most useful hospitals of the metropolis will, we are sure, never be forgotten by the citizens of Dublin and the poor of Ireland.

Months after the ceremony, in the summer of 1864, Lady Wilde wrote to a friend that 'so many dinners and invitations followed on our receiving the title to congratulate us that we have lived in a while of dissipation – now we are quiet – all the world has left town – and I begin to think of reawakening my soul'.

As these honours came, and all this dissipation, and as Sir William Wilde was at the height of his fame, and as Lady Wilde set about reawakening her soul, they were already being pursued by a woman called Mary Travers, who had been one of his patients. She was the daughter of Dr Robert Travers, Professor in Medical Jurisprudence at Trinity College Dublin. In July 1854, three months before Oscar Wilde was born, Mary, aged nineteen, accompanied by her mother, with whom she was seldom on speaking terms, came to William Wilde's surgery saying that she had problems with her hearing. Wilde, because he knew her father, waived his fee.

Mary was isolated. Her two brothers had emigrated to Australia and she did not have a close relationship with her father, who was separated from her mother. Once her treatment had ended, she continued to see William Wilde, who, with the agreement of her father, gave her manuscripts to correct and oversaw her informal education by recommending books to her. Soon, they began to write to each other. He took her to public events, helped her financially and included her in family outings. The Wildes saw a great deal of her over the next few years.

Mrs Wilde, he let Mary know, was keeping them under observation. This seems to have made Mary Travers uneasy, but William Wilde continued to write to her, offering evidence that there had been some falling-out between Mary and Jane Wilde and attempting to remain close to her. 'If Mrs Wilde asks you to dine,' he wrote to her, 'won't you come and be as good friends as ever?' Mary was invited to Christmas dinner with the Wildes in 1861.

It was clear, however, that William was growing tired of her. In March 1862 he paid her fare to Australia where she could join her brothers. She got as far as Liverpool, but did not board the ship to Australia. Two months later, she did the same again. In June 1862, while in the Wildes' house on Merrion Square, Mary entered Jane's bedroom unannounced. There was an argument between the two women, but it was not severe enough to prevent Mary planning to take the Wilde children on an outing a few days later. Jane later said, however, that Mary Travers did not dine with the Wildes again.

Mary wrote to William:

> *I have come to the conclusion that both you and Mrs Wilde are of*
> *one mind with regard to me, and that is, to see which will insult*
> *me the most. As to you, you have treated me as I strictly deserved*
> *but to Mrs Wilde I owe no money; therefore I am not obliged to*
> *gulp down her insults. My only regret is I allowed myself to be*
> *trampled on so long for the sake of Dr Wilde's condescension,*
> *which I shall remember with gratitude. The punishment has been*
> *severe but salutary . . . You will not be troubled by me again.*

She then sent William a photograph that Jane returned with a cold note: 'Dear Miss Travers, Dr Wilde returns your photograph. Yours very truly, Jane Wilde.'

Mary continued to write to William. When she drank a bottle of laudanum, William went with her to an apothecary in Westland Row to get an antidote and made sure that she took it. At one stage in this period, he doctored a corn on her foot, causing her to write:

> *Now, spiteful old lunatic, since you were to do something for me,*
> *please cut my corn that you did not do half before. I will keep*
> *your nose to the grinding stone while your wife is away, and*
> *when she returns, I will see her; so you had better not make a fool*
> *of me this time.*

In July 1863, Mary had a journalist friend produce a death notice for her as though it were actually a real cutting from a newspaper and sent it to Jane, who was staying in a house the Wildes owned on the seafront in Bray, south of Dublin. (Sir William built four houses there, renting out the other three.) When Jane returned to Merrion Square with the children, Mary appeared there again, confronting Jane and the children, demanding attention. She was not going to go away.

Mary Travers then wrote a pamphlet called *Florence Boyle Price; or a Warning*, using Jane's pen name Speranza. It told the story of Dr Quilp and his wife. Dr Quilp had

> a decidedly animal and sinister expression about his mouth, which was coarse and vulgar in the extreme, while his under-lip hung and protruded most unpleasantly. The upper part of his face did not redeem the lower part; his eyes were round and small – they were mean and prying and above all, they struck me as deficient in an expression I expected to find gracing a doctor's countenance . . . Mrs Quilp was an odd sort of undomestic woman. She spent the greater portion of her life in bed and except on state occasions, she was never visible to visitors.

The pamphlet described an encounter between the doctor and a female patient, Florence, in which the young woman is given chloroform. She

> rushes to the door, but is interrupted by the detected Quilp, who, flinging himself on his knees, attempts a passionate outburst of love, despair and remorse; but the horror-stricken Florence implores to be liberated from this dangerous place. She dreads to give the alarm knowing the irreparable disgrace, the everlasting ruin it will entail on the friend of her youth, the old man who is tottering over the grave. She fears he is mad, she says so, and begs to escape.

Terence de Vere White wrote of the pamphlet: 'There is no flattering description of Wilde to set against it, and even if we look at his picture our interpretation of it is influenced by Miss Travers' devastating commentary. She knew him, and she came to hate him. The insight born of hatred is horribly penetrating.'

Mary Travers had one thousand copies of the pamphlet printed and sent them to patients of William Wilde and to the Wildes' friends. Later, Jane Wilde testified:

> In October, perhaps the end of September, 1863, these pamphlets first came under my notice; one was sent to me through the post anonymously, afterwards several came; some were dropped into my letter-box, others came by post, and others again were brought by friends; we were deluged with them; one came through the post simply folded, so that anyone could read it; this continued for many months; I heard that they were dropped on the Rathmines road . . .

This was at a time when William Wilde's public status had never been higher but despite this – or perhaps spurred on by it – Mary Travers remained fully active in trying to embarrass him. She wrote to him demanding twenty pounds, adding: 'You will see what will happen if you are not so prompt as usual.' In February 1864, Willie and Oscar Wilde, then aged eleven and nine respectively, were sent to Portora Royal School near Enniskillen in County Fermanagh. 'They are rapidly growing into young men,' Jane wrote to a friend, 'and are both clever and good.'

In April, as Sir William was to give a lecture at the Metropolitan Hall in Dublin called 'Ireland Past and Present: The Land and the People', the audience was met with five newsboys holding large placards with the words: 'Sir William Wilde and Speranza'. They were advertising the pamphlet with the help of a handbell from an auctioneer's. Mary Travers sat in a cab close by watching proceedings. The boys shouted out: 'Sir William Wilde's letters' and sold the pamphlets for a penny each. The flysheet of the pamphlets declared that 'The writer parades Sir W. Wilde's cowardice before the public.' On other flysheets there were extracts from seventeen of Sir William's letters to Mary Travers, letters that suggested their relationship had moved beyond that normally associated with a doctor and his patient.

That evening when the Wildes returned to Merrion Square they found that a further copy of the pamphlet had been delivered with a note: 'Sold at the Music Hall on last Wednesday, the proceeds to pay the expenses of an extended edition.' The press the following day devoted more space to the events outside the hall than to the contents of Sir William's lecture. When Jane fled to Bray, Mary Travers followed her there and had a boy deliver a copy of the pamphlet to every house in her street. The boy made things worse by calling to the Wildes' house as well. He was sent away, but returned the next day with pamphlets and a placard with the names of Sir William Wilde and Speranza on it. Jane snatched a pamphlet and the placard. Mary retaliated by taking an action against Jane in a local court for larceny.

Jane responded on 6 May by writing a letter to Mary's father that read:

> *Sir – You may not be aware of the disreputable conduct of your daughter in Bray, where she consorts with all the low newspaper boys in the place, employing them to disseminate offensive placards, in which my name is given, and also tracts, in which she makes it appear that she has had an intrigue with Sir William Wilde. If she chooses to disgrace herself that is not my affair; but as her object in insulting me is the hope of extorting money, for which she has several times applied to Sir William Wilde, with threats of more annoyance if not given, I think it right to inform you that no threat of additional insult shall ever extort money for her at our hands. The wages of disgrace she has so basely treated for and demanded shall never be given to her.*

When, three weeks later, Mary Travers saw this letter, she sued for libel, demanding £2,000 in damages, with Sir William Wilde as co-defendant, since he was responsible in law for any civil wrong committed by his wife. The Wildes decided not to settle, and the case opened on 12 December 1864, lasted six days and was widely reported. Among the lawyers representing Mary Travers was the Wildes' old friend, the formidable Isaac Butt, recently returned from London. While John B. Yeats quoted a lawyer who said: 'Butt had more good feelings than any man I ever met, but he had no principle,' Terence de Vere White, who also wrote a biography of Isaac Butt, wrote:

> Wilde was not a universal favourite by any means, and Butt may not even have liked him. In any event, Butt would have regarded it as a lapse from professional standards, which he always upheld, to refuse aid to an injured party for personal reasons. He cannot have approved of his client's conduct, but he was probably persuaded that Wilde had treated her badly and that her crazy behaviour was the consequence of that ill-treatment.

Mary Travers's most damaging allegation was that Sir William Wilde, while treating her for a burn mark on her neck in his surgery in October 1862, had given her chloroform and had raped her while she was unconscious. According to the report of the court proceedings:

> He removed her bonnet for the purposes of looking at her throat . . . He pressed against her very tightly, so forcibly that she said, 'You are suffocating me.' 'I will,' he said, 'suffocate you – I can't help it.' She told the court she lost consciousness and woke when water was flung in her face and was told that if she did not rouse herself it would be his ruin and hers as well.

Mary was asked by Isaac Butt: 'Are you now able to state from anything you have observed or know, whether, in the interval of unconsciousness you have described, your person was violated?' Mary answered: 'Yes.' Butt asked: 'Was it?' Mary again answered: 'Yes.'

Sections from the letters between Mary and Sir William were read out to the court in which they seemed to be regularly falling out and making up again. Evidence in the letters made clear that he sent her money and sometimes clothes.

While Lady Wilde agreed to go into the witness box, Sir William did not. Butt cross-examined Jane for half a day, as she displayed indifference to the whole matter of her husband's relationship to Mary Travers. Butt even tried to raise the matter of the immoral tone of a novel that Jane had translated, only to be stopped by the judge. Jane did not help her case by trying to make jokes. Referring to the mock death notice that Mary had sent her, she said: 'I think I saw her next in August 1863 – after her death.' As Terence de Vere White wrote: 'For once she should have forgotten to be grand.'

In his closing address, Isaac Butt spoke of Sir William Wilde's refusal to take the stand:

I could understand him coming into court and saying his wife wrote that letter under circumstances of strong irritation . . . I could under-stand that. It would have been a powerful appeal to the jury if that had been his course . . . Shall I call it – I must do – a cowardly plea by which he shelters himself behind his wife . . . I care not what honours may have been gathered around the name of Sir William Wilde . . . but the man who instructed his counsel to speak of the daughter of his friend, of the woman whom he outraged, as a perjurer . . . is not worthy of such consideration. It was not the part of a man. I am sorry an Irish gentleman should have acted so . . . if her story is true. If not why did Sir William Wilde not come to contradict it?

Butt's summing-up was reported by *Saunders's News-letter* as follows:

Don't be led away, for remember this, for nearly ten years she had been the worshipper of Doctor Wilde. At nineteen years of age he had attracted her as a superior being. He had insinuated himself into a knowledge of her wants, her domestic grievances, and the poverty of her home, alienated her from her mother, and taught her to be dissatisfied with her clergyman.

Butt spoke about the power Sir William had over Mary since their first meeting: 'From that hour she became his slave as completely as Zelica became the slave of the Veiled Prophet . . . The plaintiff had done things which no man can justify, but who made her do so? She was a girl of nineteen when she was brought by her mother to him and submitted to his care.'

He described Sir William as 'a moral chloroform that stupefied her faculties, surprised her senses in the terrible scene, left her senseless and prostrate at the feet of her destroyer'.

Butt said of Mary Travers:

> I believe that unconsciously she was in love with Sir William Wilde . . . It was hinted at the other side that she was his mistress, but that was not true, his letters showed it was untrue . . . She was driven away from the house of him whose secret she had kept – he, whose guilt she had concealed . . . the various acts and publications charged against her were but the utterances of a broken heart . . . Will you condemn her, while the man who asks you by your oaths to believe he is perjured, shrinks from coming in here and pledging his oaths to that to which he asks twelve Irish gentlemen to pledge theirs?

The judge, in his summing-up, said that the correspondence between Sir William and Mary Travers 'was of a very extraordinary character to take place between a married man and a girl of her attractions'. He added that if her allegations of rape had been the subject of a criminal prosecution, they would have been thrown out of any court because of her failure to report them at the time and her continuing to correspond with Wilde and receive favours from him and be in his company.

The jury, after a short deliberation, decided that Mary Travers had been libelled in the letter Lady Wilde wrote to her father. While damages were set at just a farthing, the verdict meant that the Wildes were responsible for costs, which amounted to £2,000, almost quarter of a million pounds in today's money. *The Irish Times* concluded: 'Thus ended a suit that shook society in Dublin like a thunderclap.'

★

In Reading Gaol, the regime was not as severe as it had been in Pentonville and Wandsworth, where Oscar Wilde had spent the first months of his imprisonment. He did not, for example, have to do hard manual labour in Reading. He was assigned work in the garden and was put in charge of bringing books to other prisoners. While he took enormous exception to Colonel Isaacson, the governor of Reading during the early part of his stay, stating, with his usual flair for phrasing, that the colonel had 'the eyes of a ferret, the body of an ape, and the soul of a rat', he grew to admire Major J. O. Nelson, who replaced Isaacson in July 1896 when Wilde still had ten months of his sentence to serve. It was Nelson who was in charge when Wilde wrote *De Profundis* in his cell.

That Sunday afternoon, as I kept reading from *De Profundis*, I did not check the time or take a break. I tried not to stumble over the Greek words with which Wilde had peppered the text. The tone moved from the ruminative, the speculative to the most intimate and confessional and private. It was hard not to imagine him lying back on his plank bed and realizing that there were certain things about his life and the life of his family that Lord Alfred Douglas did not know and did not need to know. It is impossible, for example, that Oscar Wilde returned to Merrion

Square from Portora in December 1864 for his Christmas holidays and did not hear about what had happened in the court during the weeks before.

What is remarkable is how many connections there are between the case of Mary Travers versus Lady Wilde and the case that Oscar Wilde took against the Marquess of Queensberry. First, there was the frenetic, fearless, almost manic activity of both Travers and Queensberry, who sought to embarrass and harass in public and private Sir William and Oscar Wilde respectively, both of whom were becoming increasingly famous and feeling more and more unassailable. The image of Mary Travers outside the lecture that Sir William was to give is close to the image of the Marquess of Queensberry attempting to disrupt the opening night of *The Importance of Being Earnest* in 1895. Both wished to use a grand, ceremonious occasion for maximum dramatic effect.

Both Travers and Queensberry also left printed accusations for everyone to read, the former a pamphlet, the latter the 'posing as a somdomite' card at Oscar Wilde's club. Both controversies centred on a long and turbulent sexual relationship between one of the Wildes and a younger person. Both controversies suggested that this person had been corrupted by one of the Wildes. Both controversies also included a libel action. In both cases, the lawyer for the other side was someone whom the Wildes knew. Although Oscar Wilde did not know Edward Carson, who represented the Marquess of Queensberry, as well as his parents had known Isaac Butt, they had been at Trinity College Dublin together. 'No doubt he will perform his task with the added bitterness of an old friend,' Wilde said when he heard that Carson was to take the brief. Both Butt and Carson, ambitious men who later became influential politicians, attempted to use a book to suggest to the jury that the witness's morals were suspect: the first that novel translated by Lady Wilde, the second *The Picture of Dorian Gray*. Both Lady Wilde and her son made jokes and attempted a superior tone in the witness box. In each instance, the main focus of the case, Sir William Wilde and Oscar, had two young sons who were away at school as the court proceedings took place.

Of much more importance, however, are the differences between the two, especially the differences in the outcomes. While Oscar went to prison and was ostracized by polite society, many in the medical establishment supported Sir William in the aftermath of the court case, as Emer O'Sullivan emphasized in *The Fall of the House of Wilde*. For example, on Christmas Eve 1864, the Irish correspondent of *The Lancet* devoted an editorial to the conclusion of the trial:

> Sir William Wilde has to congratulate himself that he has passed through an ordeal supported by the sympathies of the entire mass of his professional brethren in this city; that he has been acquitted of a charge as disgraceful as it was unexpected, even without having to stoop to the painful necessity of contradicting it upon oath in the witness box, by the expressed opinion of one of the ablest of our judges, by the verdict of a most intelligent special jury, by the unanimous opinion of his fellow citizens, and by, what I am sure he will not value least, that of every member of his own profession.

Four days earlier, however, *The Times* in London, while expressing sympathy with Lady Wilde, did not take the same lenient view of his behaviour:

> She [Mary Travers] did not deny that she had received money from Sir William even subsequently to the time of the alleged offence, but she also maintained that though she had asked for money, it had been freely offered, and sometimes returned. The general conclusion, in short, to be drawn from her evidence . . . is that Sir William, having originally been introduced to her in his professional capacity, had taken a great interest in her affairs, had wished to befriend her, and

had gradually placed himself on terms of intimacy which were afterwards abused. She then retaliated as best she could in the manner which induced Lady Wilde to interfere.

Lady Wilde wrote to a Swedish friend, pointing out that

*Miss Travers is half mad. She was very destitute and haunted our house to borrow money and we were very kind to her as we pitied her – but suddenly she took a dislike to me amounting to hatred. It was very annoying, but of course no one believed her story. All Dublin now calls on us to offer their sympathy, and all the medical Profession here and in London have sent letters expressing their disbelief of the (in fact) impossible charge. Sir Wm will not be injured by it and the best proof is that his professional hours were never so occupied as now . . . happily all is over now and our enemy has been signally defeated in her efforts to injure us.*

The case also brought Isaac Butt 'a flood of business', according to his biographer: 'In one day alone he was handed seventeen briefs. He was very pleased.'

The Travers court case did not seem to affect the lives of the Wildes in any obvious way. They were invited, for example, to the ball at the Lord Mayor's to meet the Prince of Wales when he came to Dublin in May 1865. In May 1870 Sir William was among the distinguished and varied group that attended a meeting in a Dublin hotel addressed by Isaac Butt to form a Home Government Association in Ireland. And in 1873 Sir William received the Cunningham Medal from the Royal Irish Academy, its highest honour.

It is possible that the court case was seen as another symptom of what fame meant, just as Lady Wilde's efforts to be prosecuted in 1848 added to her notoriety, but caused her no apparent harm.

By 1871, Charles Gavan Duffy, at whose trial she had attempted to intervene, had become Premier of Victoria in Australia. In Ireland in the second half of the nineteenth century, political prisoners were slowly coming to be seen as heroes. As William Murphy wrote in *Political Imprisonment and the Irish, 1912–1921*:

> prison was transformed into a pulpit, a soapbox, a stage and, providing one survived, time served as a political prisoner became an important qualification for public life in Ireland . . . The lesson was not lost on ambitious men. By early March 1889 twenty-four sitting Irish MPs had been imprisoned at least once, and this trend continued . . . Isaac Butt's presidency of the Amnesty Association, established in 1869 to campaign for the release of Fenian prisoners, provided him with the base from which to launch the Home Government Association in 1870 and to become an MP in 1871.

In 1882 in America, Oscar Wilde gave a lecture entitled 'The Irish Poets of 1848' and remembered the Young Irelanders, the so-called 'Men of '48', coming to parties in his parents' house. These included not only Gavan Duffy but also John Mitchel, whose *Jail Journal* was published in 1854, the year of Oscar Wilde's birth, and William Smith O'Brien, who had been sentenced to death in 1848. When the sentence was commuted, Smith O'Brien was transported to Tasmania, returning to Ireland in 1856.

This is not to suggest that the allegations made against Sir William Wilde in 1864 and the libel action against his wife were in any way political. The case was personal, sexual, intimate. But it does suggest that the experience of court and then prison was something that had been normalized or even fetishized in the house on Merrion Square where Oscar Wilde was raised. In the soirées that his parents gave, the idea of loyalty, whether to the crown or to Victorian sexual mores, was never stable.

This instability may have made conversation more glittering, and, since his best characters obey no rules, it may have nourished the later work Wilde did as a dramatist, but it did not help him once he had to stand in an English witness box, when he, unlike his parents, was facing an actual prison sentence.

Of all the differences that Oscar Wilde established in *De Profundis* between his family and that of Lord Alfred Douglas, the opposing views of what court appearance and prison meant were perhaps the most profound. In the tone Wilde used in what he wrote in that cell in the early months of 1897, there is a sense of shock at discovering the difference between prison as something imagined and then something that became desperately real for him when, at the age of forty, he found himself sentenced. In February 1897, as Wilde was writing *De Profundis*, Major Nelson remarked to Wilde's friend Robert Ross: 'He looks well. But like all men unused to manual labour who receive a sentence of this kind, he will be dead within two years.'

Wilde, in fact, survived for three and a half years after his release. His father lived for more than eleven years after the Mary Travers libel action. In 1867, Sir William published *Lough Corrib, Its Shores and Islands*, which is his most relaxed and engaging book. As he travelled by steamboat along the shores of the lake and then meticulously studied the landscape close to the house he had built at Moytura, he displayed his enquiring mind, his enthusiasm and his knowledge. He was not a great writer, but rather someone who managed to show himself as a great talker as he wrote. The pages were filled with a tremendous and absorbing sense of his own presence, as he measured old ruins or offered his theories about building practices or complained about how badly kept important old buildings were.

In explaining why certain churches were not aligned east–west as they should be, for example, he offered the ingenious idea that the builders, 'in laying out these churches, were guided by the sun's rising and setting at the time of the year in which the building was commenced'.

When he found himself among the ruins of the medieval

Franciscan friary of Ross Errilly, he was ready to be both seduced by the atmosphere and appalled by the level of neglect:

> Wandering among these noble ruins, evincing so much taste, if not luxury, one cannot help peopling them, in imagination, with the inmates of four or five hundred years gone by; when, after dinner, the brown-robed friars strolled in the adjoining cloisters, of which several of the arches are quite perfect. But the picture dims as we proceed from that portion of the ruins allocated to the creature comforts of the clergy . . . for passing into the great church by its western entrance, amidst heaps of human skulls and bones, into the great aisle or nave, we are at once met by droves of sheep and oxen, that rush from off the altars, or from out of the tombs, or from within the precincts of the small chapels around us.

Some of Wilde's lists and descriptions in this, his last book, were brilliant. For example, he wrote about the amount of water in the vicinity of Cong in County Mayo:

> There is water everywhere – gliding by in the broad river; gushing from the surrounding rocks; boiling up in vast pools that supply several mills; oozing through the crevices of stones; rising in the interior of caverns; appearing and disappearing wherever its wayward nature wills; passing in and out everywhere, except where man tried to turn it – into the monster dry canal.

As with his Boyne book, William Wilde noted the differences between Ireland and England; he understood that efforts to conquer Ireland in the name of the crown were essentially doomed, almost from the start:

> The people were . . . poor, and likewise ignorant, improvident, and uneducated, although far superior to the same class in the sister

country; but they were disloyal – not so much on account of Prot-
estantism, tithes, Catholic disabilities, the want of educational
resources, or any other real or sentimental grievance, but because
they had never been conquered by either force, justice or kindness.

In his wildly colourful speech on the Aran Islands, he was sure
that he had invited his guests to dine at the site of 'the last
standing-place of the Firbolg aborigines of Ireland, here to fight
their last battle if driven to the western surge, or, as I have already
pointed out to you, to take a fearful and eternal departure from
the rocks they had contested foot by foot'. He admitted, however, that 'of that race we have no written knowledge'.

In his Corrib book, he mentioned 'the battle of Moytura,
stated by the bards, and believed by the early writers (where they
assign dates to events), to have been fought in the year of the
world 3303'. Later in the book, he gave a forty-page vivid description of the battle as it took place. He wrote almost as though he
had been a witness. He moved us moment by moment through
what happened over the four days of the battle and inch by inch
through the landscape in which it took place. As with his version
of the history of Dun Aengus on the Aran Islands, it all made
sense until none of it did, since all of it was based on legend and
supposition. As Terence de Vere White wrote, Wilde

was using his old friend John O'Donovan's translation of the
unpublished manuscript [of 'The Book of Invasions'] (in the
library of Trinity College) for his account of the battle. It lived in
his memory and he never tired of trying to identify the various
places, speculating on the circles of flat stones like miniature
Stonehenges that abound in the district.

William Wilde must have been marvellous company as he
tramped through these ancient sites. His interest in locating a

precise site for a legendary event was not unusual, it should be pointed out. Less than a decade after Wilde published his Corrib book, a German archaeologist, using Homer's *Iliad* as a source, claimed to have found ancient Mycenae and the tomb of Clytemnestra.

However, there were times in his Corrib book when he allowed himself to be hesitant and careful about the origin and purpose of what he had discovered. Close to Inishmain Abbey, for example, he unearthed a solid structure formed of undressed stone with openings, like crypts, cut into it: 'These crypts are certainly the most remarkable and inexplicable structures that have yet been discovered in Ireland. At top they are formed somewhat like the roof of a high-pitched Gothic church, with long stone ribs or rafters abutting upon a low side wall, and meeting each other at top.'

What is fascinating here is a footnote that contains a simple sentence: 'Subsequent to its discovery by the author and his son Oscar, in August 1866, and after Mr Wakeman had taken drawings of it, the Earl of Dunraven had a very perfect photograph taken of the western face of this structure.' In the main text, Wilde resumes his speculation about the function of the building: 'Possibly it may have been a prison, or penitentiary, in which some of the refractory brethren of the neighbouring abbey were confined.' There is also an illustration included in the book of an enclosure on an artificial island on Lough Mask, which Sir William Wilde said is 'by Master Wilde'.

Oscar Wilde was eleven then, almost twelve, and would have been on holidays from Portora. This picture of him wandering on a remote island in the west of Ireland with his father, seeking out ancient buildings that had not been noticed or charted, and making drawings, is a new version of him, far away from the London he eventually moved to, far from the parties and gatherings, the witticisms ('Nature: a place where birds fly around uncooked'), the cosmopolitan jibes ('Grass is hard and lumpy and damp, and full of dreadful black insects. Why, even Morris's poorest workman could make you a more comfortable seat than the whole of Nature can').

Wilde knew about grass and birds. On his holidays from Oxford, he spent time at Moytura and at Illaunroe Lodge. In August 1876, he wrote to his friend Reginald Harding, beginning the letter 'Dear Kitten':

> *Frank Miles and I came down here last week and had a very royal time of it sailing. We were at the top of Lough Corrib which if you refer to your geography, you will find to be a lake thirty miles long, ten broad and situated among the most romantic scenery in Ireland . . . On Friday we go into Connemara to a charming little fishing-lodge we have in the mountains where I hope to make him land a salmon and kill a brace of grouse . . . I expect to have very good sport indeed this season.*

Since Miles was a painter, Oscar Wilde did a painting too, a watercolour of the view from Moytura House.

Later in August, he wrote to William Ward from Illaunroe Lodge, Connemara:

> *I have only got one salmon as yet but have had heaps of sea trout which give great play. I have not had a blank day yet. Grouse are few but I have got a lot of hares so have had a capital time of it. I hope that next year you and 'The Kitten' will come and stay a (lunar) month with me. I am sure that you would like this wild mountainous country close to the Atlantic and teeming with sport of all kinds. It is in every way magnificent and makes me years younger than actual history records.*

Sir William Wilde had died the previous April, at the age of sixty-one. Crowds attended his funeral, even Isaac Butt was among the mourners. His daughter Isola had died in 1867, shortly before her tenth birthday. And in 1871, Sir William's other two daughters, Emily and Mary, aged twenty-four and twenty-two, were burned to death in a fire. John B. Yeats wrote to his son the poet that Sir William attended the funeral and he had been told that 'his groans could be heard by people outside the house'. He added: 'there is a tragedy all the more intense, because it had to be buried in silence. It was not allowed to give sorrow words.' In the inquiry into their deaths, their names were given as 'Wylie' rather than 'Wilde'. The name Wilde, however, was on their gravestones.

In the aftermath of these deaths, William Wilde had done less medical work and spent more and more time in Moytura. When he died, his fortune was much depleted. Many of the properties he owned had been mortgaged. Lady Wilde wrote to Oscar: 'How are we all to live? It is all a muddle. My opinion is that all that is coming to us will be swallowed up in our borrowings before we are paid.'

In June 1877, Oscar wrote to Reginald Harding from Merrion Square: 'I am very much down in spirits and depressed. A cousin of ours to whom we were all very attached has just died – quite suddenly from some chill caught riding. I dined with him on Saturday and he was dead on Wednesday.' The cousin was in fact Henry Wilson, William Wilde's first illegitimate child. In his will he left most of his money to the hospital his father had founded and where he had worked. He left Willie Wilde £8,000, and left Oscar Wilde, whom he felt to be close to converting to Roman Catholicism, only £100, on condition of his remaining a Protestant. Henry and Oscar had inherited Illaunroe from their father and Wilde now also inherited Henry's half-share, on condition that he did not become a Catholic for five years. 'You see I suffer a good deal from my Romish leanings,' Oscar wrote, 'in pocket and mind . . . Fancy a man going before "God and the Eternal Silences" with his wretched Protestant prejudices and bigotry clinging to him still.'

The following summer Oscar Wilde wrote a letter to the Jesuit Father Matthew Russell from Illaunroe. The last paragraph read: 'I am resting here in the mountains – great peace and quiet everywhere – and hope to send you a sonnet as a result.' That seems to be the last time he went there. In 1881, to keep his life in London going, Wilde mortgaged the property and three years later he sold it.

Before Oscar Wilde arrived in London, however, when he was seeking an archaeological studentship at Oxford in 1879, he wrote to A. H. Sayce, Professor of Comparative Philology: 'I think it would suit me very well – as I have done a good deal of travelling already and from my boyhood have been accustomed, through my father, to visiting and reporting on ancient sites, taking rubbings and measurements and all techniques of open-air archaeologica. It is a subject of intense interest to me.' As Richard Ellmann wrote in *Four Dubliners*, 'In the process by which Oscar Wilde became Oscar Wilde, his parents must be allowed to have given their impetus.' In the moments when the young Oscar Wilde appears in his father's Corrib book, and in this letter, and in the letters he wrote from Illaunroe in the summer after his father's death, we can catch a glimpse of the impetus Oscar Wilde received from his father, an impetus that suggests a sort of shadow path for him, a path that, as he sought fame in England, he did not follow.

There is a word his father uses twice in his Corrib book, to describe a type of ornamentation. It is the word 'fleur-de-lis'. It is used first to describe the decoration on two tombstones William Wilde had uncovered at Annaghdown and later in a description of two tomb flags at Cong.

It is strange how the word slips and moves and echoes and makes its way into the letter that Oscar Wilde wrote in his cell thirty years later.

The word 'fleur-de-lis' came in the form of a ballad that Lord Alfred Douglas had written in the year before Wilde was imprisoned. It was called 'Jonquil and Fleur-de-lys'. In the poem, two boys meet, the first a shepherd and the other the son of a king, and in a mild homoerotic game they decide to switch identities:

> And after that they did devise
> For mirth and sport, that each should wear
> The other's clothes, and in this guise
> Make play each other's parts to bear.
>
> Whereon they stripped off all their clothes,
> And when they stood up in the sun,
> They were as like as one white rose
> On one green stalk, to another one.

In the January before he went to prison, Wilde, in an interview, said that his three comedies to date were to each other 'as a wonderful young poet has beautifully said – "as one white rose / On one green stalk, to another one"'. He used 'Fleur-de-lys' as an affectionate nickname for Douglas.

When Lord Alfred Douglas realized that Wilde was to be declared bankrupt and thus would be visited in prison by a solicitor's clerk, he sent him a message that, in the presence of the warder, was actually conveyed to Wilde in a low voice by the clerk: 'Prince Fleur-de-Lys wishes to be remembered to you.'

In *De Profundis*, Wilde wrote:

I stared at him. He repeated the message again. I did not know what he meant. 'The gentleman is abroad at present,' he added mysteriously. It all flashed across me, and I remember that, for the first and last time in my entire prison life, I laughed. In that laugh was all the scorn of all the world. Prince Fleur-de-Lys! I saw – and subsequent events showed me that I rightly saw – that nothing that had happened had made you realize a single thing. You were

in your own eyes still the graceful prince of a trivial comedy, not
the sombre figure of a tragic show.

Although Jonquil in Douglas's version of things was a shepherd
lad and Fleur-de-Lys the son of a king, and they both became each
other, this was not the story of Wilde and Douglas. Rather, this
doubling and merging happened within Wilde's own complex
spirit. He merged the talents he had taken from his parents with
their sense of nobility and their feeling that they could do whatever
they liked. And then, in his own imagination and in his own books
and plays, he doubled what he had inherited from them and
became, as he wrote in *De Profundis*, 'a lord of language'.

In the dim light of his cell, almost a hundred and twenty years
after he wrote *De Profundis*, as I came to the end of my reading, it
was hard not to feel awe at the idea of how far he had come, what
dark knowledge he had gained, and how much he understood –
as his father had understood after his court case when he wrote
his book on Lough Corrib – that the only way he could rescue
himself was by writing. Thus in this cell each day, Oscar Wilde
was busy, as his parents had been, finding the right words. He was
working, finishing the letter so that it could be handed to him as
he emerged into daylight on 19 May 1897.

*John B. Yeats: The Playboy of West Twenty-Ninth Street*

Somewhere in the great, unsteady archive where our souls will be held, there is a special section that records the quality of our gaze. The stacks in this branch of the archive will preserve for posterity the history of those moments when a look or a glance intensified, when watchfulness opened out or narrowed in, due to curiosity or desire or suspicion or fear. Maybe that is what we remember most of each other – the face of the other glancing up, the second when we are held in someone else's gaze.

The idea of gaze does not come to us simply. It is not stable. In the poems of W. B. Yeats, for example, when the word appears, it is often in different contexts. In his early poem 'The Two Trees', the poet calls on his beloved to gaze inwards, to 'gaze in thine own heart' in the first and last line of the opening stanza, and in the second stanza the poem proposes that the gaze outward at the disturbing world is to be avoided:

> Gaze no more in the bitter glass
> The demons, with their subtle guile,
> Lift up before us when they pass . . .

In 'The Folly of Being Comforted', Yeats evokes a time when his love had all the wild summer in her gaze. In 'Aedh Tells of the Perfect Beauty', he allows the gaze to be personal and beguiling:

> The poets labouring all their days
> To build a perfect beauty in rhyme
> Are overthrown by a woman's gaze . . .

In 'The Second Coming', however, the idea of the gaze is dangerous, frightening, speaking of a world to come in which all comfort will be shattered by

> A shape with lion body and the head of a man,
> A gaze blank and pitiless as the sun . . .

*

In June 2004 I was in the Special Collections section of the library of Union College in Schenectady in upstate New York when I heard one of the librarians telling someone on the telephone in a half-whisper that someone with my name was in looking at the correspondence of John B. Yeats, which had been transcribed and donated to the library by William M. Murphy.

An hour later, I looked up from my reading of the Yeats letters to find a man gazing at me. It struck me immediately who he was. It was William M. Murphy himself, the author of *Prodigal Father*, a biography of John B. Yeats, and *Family Secrets*, a book about the Yeats family.

As he watched me, the image of another gaze came into my mind. It was a decade earlier, an early summer's evening in Dublin, and I was walking home along Capel Street when I saw the novelist John McGahern coming towards me in the distance on the same side of the street. As he spotted me, he held my gaze. For a few minutes as we walked towards each other, it was as though we were meeting somewhere in the countryside, with just fields or a lane between us. Neither of us smiled or gestured, but neither of us looked away. When he finally was eye to eye with me, after a brief conversation, he asked me if I was going anywhere special and when I said that I was not, he suggested that I would turn and walk back towards Dame Street with him and we could have dinner in Nico's.

Our friendship was based on the fact that we both liked books and enjoyed talking about them. He tended to read the same books over and over, and took pleasure in expressing his insights into and deep appreciation for the very few books that had met with his approval. One of these books was William M. Murphy's *Prodigal Father*, and another was a volume of John B. Yeats's letters. He liked how good-humoured and tolerant Murphy's book was, how well written, and how much sympathy it contained. (We both marvelled over individual sentences in the book, such as 'By the end of 1897, Lady Gregory had lined up all the Yeatses she thought important – the three men – for further management.')

McGahern also loved Yeats's letters for their fresh thinking and their charm, their openness to life, their readiness to accept no easy truth. When his French publisher asked him to select an Irish book that had never been translated into French, McGahern chose an edition of these letters and wrote an introduction to it.

In John Butler Yeats's letters there was great wit ('I think lots of men die of their wives and *thousands* of women die of their husbands,' for example, or 'I wrote to Willie some time ago and said it was as bad to be a poet's father as the intimate friend of George Moore') and large-hearted tenderness ('Without imagination – and of the kind that creates – there is no love, whether it be love of a girl or love of a country or love of one's friend or even of children, and of our wives'). He had original things to say about being old in New York ('old men are popular here, in the streets and everywhere, a breezy sort of popularity, as if they thought it was jolly to be old and to have so long survived pneumonia and cancer and consumption and drink, and all the evils flesh is heir to'). And rude things to say about Bostonians:

*They are always careful of their dollars. The richer they are the worse they are. And then they are so pleased with themselves. They don't know that in my eyes they are dirt. They hate England intensely. That is the only interesting thing about them. I am told by*

> *everyone that it is terrible to live in Boston, it is so infernally dull. I*
> *suppose they have a good side but I have not as yet discovered it.*

While McGahern's gaze, when he spoke about these letters, was frank and straightforward, polite and mannerly, there was also something stern in it, and something withheld. The suggestion was that he looked inwards as much as outwards. But, since he had been a schoolmaster, there was a sense too from his gaze that he noticed everything and he would forget very little.

William Murphy's gaze, on the other hand, was softer, but also more guarded and quizzical. As I watched him from my desk in the library of Union College, I realized what his problem was. If he came over and found that I was in Schenectady for a few days, with evenings free, he might feel that he had to invite me to his home for supper or for a drink. He seemed, as he stood there, to be weighing up the consequences of that.

In other words, quietly and carefully, he was trying to ascertain, just by looking, if I might be someone who would frighten his dogs, or undo his lawn, or spread false and malicious rumours about him and his family when I got back to Ireland, or tell him and his wife the long and melancholy story of my next novel.

In order to put him out of his misery, I stood up and walked towards him and thanked him for the great work he had done on the Yeats family and for depositing his papers in the library. And then, as his gaze further softened into a look of kindness and ease, he invited me to have supper the following evening.

At the table with him and his wife, I discovered that they both had the same charm and good humour and tolerant view of the world as *Prodigal Father* did. He spoke warmly of other, younger biographers, such as Roy Foster and Adrian Frazier, who had approached the same material. Among the many suggestions he made that evening was that, when I was in Dublin again, I should go and see Michael Yeats, the son of the poet, who might be glad to meet someone who was interested in his grandfather as much as his father, and also to spend time with someone who was brought up, as I was, in a Fianna Fáil family – Fianna Fáil being at the time the main political party in Ireland, but also a political movement that was unfashionable, to say the least, and an organization that very few Yeats scholars knew anything about. Michael Yeats had been a Fianna Fáil senator and a member of the European Parliament for the party, of which my father had also been a loyal member.

Thus a few months later, I found myself having lunch with Michael Yeats and his wife, Gráinne, at Cliff House, their home in Dalkey in the suburbs of Dublin. While Michael's gaze was hooded and guarded, his wife often gave me a beady glance across the table. She was used to people coming to the house looking for something. All I wanted, however, was to see some sketches towards a self-portrait that John B. Yeats had made in New York at the end of his life.

After lunch, Michael Yeats motioned me to follow him out to a hallway with a stairway leading to a floor below. He opened a long drawer in an old chest of drawers and began to rummage until he found, wrapped in tissue paper, some unframed drawings by his grandfather, self-portraits done in old age. As soon as he removed the tissue paper and put them on a table, the face of his grandfather looked out at us, filled with urgent life. The gaze was vivid, piercing, questioning, the gaze of a spirit that was fully alert both to its own power and to the fierce amount of inner energy that lay behind it.

For as long as I thought polite, I looked at these drawings, remembering how Lady Gregory had remarked that, since John B. Yeats had so much difficulty finishing paintings, then he should be encouraged to do as many drawings as possible, drawings that could be done in one sitting.

As I turned, my eye was instantly caught by a long oil painting that was hanging on the stairwell. For a second, I thought it had to be a reproduction, since I thought that the original, having been owned by the New York lawyer and collector John Quinn, was in the United States. But as I looked more closely, I realized that this was the actual self-portrait that Yeats had worked on for the last decade of his life.

It was commissioned by John Quinn in New York in 1911 and worked on between then and the artist's death in 1922. In 1919, Yeats wrote to Quinn: 'It is like watching a blessed ghost of a long lost beloved slowly materialising. I think of nothing else and I dream of it.' It was done in Yeats's small bedroom, also his studio, at his boarding house on West Twenty-Ninth Street. Mary Colum described in her autobiography the iron bed and cheap worn rug, and the easel on which was 'always erected a portrait at which he tinkered day after day'.

John B. Yeats's preoccupation with this late self-portrait accounts for its heavily worked surface, as he often scraped off and reworked what he had done. It was part of his restless, paradoxical spirit that he would spend more than a decade on a single image so that he could all the more capture a sense of spontaneity.

It made me think of a moment from a letter written in 1906 from Yeats to his son William, quoted by William Murphy in his book:

> *I think every work of art should* survive *after all the labour bestowed on it, and* survive as a sketch. *To the last it must be something struck off at a first heat. This is the meaning of impressionism. I have lately been reading Shakespeare's* Cleopatra *and it has all the pregnancy of a sketch, because it is a sketch. The details are not filled in. No conscientious labour has been spent on it. It is all a riot and extravagance. Now, the essence of a sketch is that it leaves much to the imagination.*

In his preface to *Early Memories*, W. B. Yeats wrote how his father in his letters 'constantly spoke about this picture as his masterpiece, insisted again and again . . . that he had found what he had been seeking all his life'. In a letter to a friend in January 1917, John B. Yeats wrote: 'Now I mean as soon as possible to finish my portrait, on which I have been working for many years . . . I want it to be "great" – an immortal work – that's why I put off finishing it.' The painting also became one of Yeats's excuses in old age for not returning to Ireland since he insisted that the self-portrait in progress 'must not be endangered by a change of light'.

Now, in the scarce light of this landing, this painting, which was still unfinished at the time of the artist's death, had come home to Ireland. As I stood there, I gazed at his gaze, a gaze even more arresting and engaging than the ones in the drawings. It was like something in motion rather than fixed; it suggested a deep originality of spirit. It was a portrait of someone who had been lit up by life. Filled with curiosity itself and vitality, it provoked a response. It made you want to know who this man was.

John B. Yeats, the son of a clergyman, was born in a village in County Down, where his father was rector, in 1839. While his father had a good income, he had also inherited land in Kilkenny through the Butler connection on his grandmother's side. Of his childhood, Yeats would later write to his son: 'In those days it was considered bad manners for parents to speak crossly to their children, and so we grew up in what I might call the discipline of good manners as contrasted with the discipline of good morals.'

Having attended a couple of boarding schools, Yeats entered Trinity College Dublin, as his father had done. By this time, his parents had moved to Dublin and were living in Sandymount, and, as good Anglo-Irish Protestants, they were moving easily in the best Dublin society. As a student, Yeats often joined his parents to dine at the house of Sir William and Lady Wilde, as his son would later dine at the house of Oscar Wilde in London. Isaac Butt had been a college classmate of his father and remained a close friend, close enough for John B. Yeats's father to call his youngest son Isaac Butt Yeats.

Since two brothers from Sligo, Charles and George Pollexfen, whose family owned a shipping and milling business, were among Yeats's best friends at school, and he, who was charming and open in his manners, had found their seriousness, indeed their sullenness, interesting and beguiling, he made a visit to them in Sligo while at Trinity. The town of Sligo, he later wrote, 'was strange to me and very beautiful in the deepening twilight . . . Dublin and my uneasy life there and Trinity College, though but a short day's journey, were obliterated . . .'

While staying with the Pollexfens, he met their sister Susan, whom he would marry in 1863. Years later, when he tried to explain his decision to marry her, Yeats said that her family genius 'for being dismal' was, he felt, what he needed. 'Indeed it was because of this I took to them and married my wife. I thought I would place myself under prison rules and learn all the virtues.'

After Trinity, Yeats studied to become a barrister, but, in fact, spent most of his time with a number of literary friends, including the critic Edward Dowden and the poet John Todhunter. Despite his desultory attention to his law studies, he was elected auditor of the Debating Society at the King's Inns in Dublin. The address he gave to the society as auditor was attended by both Sir William Wilde and Isaac Butt. There is evidence that Butt, then the best-known barrister in Ireland, agreed to have young Yeats as his 'devil' (a 'devil' is a young lawyer who works with an older barrister and thus gains contacts and practical experience). Yeats liked Isaac Butt enormously, having learned, as he said, 'to judge people by their manner', which he believed 'a surer indication to character than deeds, though it may be heresy to say so'. Years after Butt's death, John B. Yeats wrote: 'Such is the charm of personality that the man who has it is forgiven, though his sins be scarlet – for instance lovable Isaac Butt.'

By this time, his first child had been born. The boy was named William Butler Yeats. Soon afterwards the Yeatses had a daughter, Lily. As a law student, John B. Yeats had begun drawing, and it was his nascent talent, as well as the influence of his literary friends and also something deep within his sensibility, that pulled him away from the law. 'I meant to succeed,' he later said. 'My will was in it, that is my conscious will.' But in his unconscious will, he wanted to become an artist.

Thus early in 1867, leaving his wife and two young children in Sligo, he set out for London and enrolled in the Heatherley School of Fine Art. His wife's family, the Pollexfens, the most practical of people, did not approve. Nor indeed did his wife. 'I don't think she approved of a single one of my ideas or theories or opinions, to her only foolishness,' he later wrote. None of this deterred him. In his unfinished memoirs, he wrote, 'The Pollexfens are as solid and powerful as the sea-cliffs, but hitherto they are altogether dumb. To give them a voice is like giving a voice to the sea-cliffs. By marriage to a Pollexfen I have given a tongue to the sea-cliffs.'

Since John B. Yeats made no money as an artist and since the tenants on his estate in Kilkenny did not always pay the rent, his growing family, including Lollie, born in 1868, and Jack, born in 1871, lived for long periods in Sligo with the Pollexfens. For example, as a boy, W. B. Yeats spent more than two years with his mother and her family in Ireland, while his father remained impecuniously in London. Yeats's youngest child, the painter Jack, lived in Sligo with his mother's family almost continuously between the ages of eight and sixteen.

Yeats's way of painting portraits was remarked on by many of his sitters. Edward Dowden, for example, described him at work:

> he gets so thoroughly into the 'fluid and attaching' state, every glance at one's face seems to give him a shock, and through a series of such shocks he progresses. He finishes nothing, but gets his whole picture just into an embryo existence, out of which it gradually emerges by a series of incalculable developments; and all the while he is indulging in endless gossip of the peculiar

*Yeatsian* kind, i.e. telling trivial facts and reducing them under laws of character founded on ethical classifications on down to Aristotle or any other student of character – classifications which are perpetually growing and dissolving.

Dowden noted that Yeats had 'a pleasant rather high-pitched but musical voice . . . a soft elusive voice' and 'one noticed the keen look in his eyes and the movement of his hands and fingers, for he had wonderful hands, not beautiful, but the long hand and finger of the sculptor and artist'.

When Yeats's family finally joined him in London, they were able to observe at close quarters the problems their father faced. In his *Autobiographies*, W. B. Yeats remembered as an eleven-year-old observing what happened to a painting of a landscape by his father: 'He began it in spring and painted all through the year, the picture changing with the seasons, and gave it up unfinished when he had painted the snow upon the heath-covered banks. He is never satisfied and can never make himself say that any picture is finished.' He recalled a stranger in London, on finding out whose son he was, remarking: 'O, that is the painter who scrapes out every day what he painted the day before.'

Nor did John B. Yeats attempt to court the famous. When Browning, who admired one of his paintings, called and left an invitation for him to visit, he did not follow it up, and, despite encouragement, he did not visit Rossetti.

In 1881, when W. B. Yeats was sixteen, the family returned to Dublin and lived in Howth, overlooking Dublin Bay. Susan Yeats was always happier in Ireland. Her son, who liked to mythologize, later wrote: 'She read no books, but she and the fisherman's wife would tell each other stories that Homer might have told, pleased with any moment of sudden intensity and laughing together over any point of satire.' But her husband, in a letter, made clear that she was deeply unhappy. 'If I showed her my real thoughts,' he wrote, 'she became quite silent and silent for days, though inwardly furious.'

Even though Yeats made no money as a painter, and was constantly in debt, his humour remained good, his optimism high and his conversation sparkling and fresh. In his *Autobiography*, published in 1936, G. K. Chesterton, who was a visitor to the Yeatses on one of their further stays in London, wrote of the son:

> William Butler Yeats might seem as solitary as an eagle; but he had a nest . . . The intensity and individualism itself could never wash out of the world's memories the general impression of Willie and Lily and Lolly and Jack: names cast backwards and forwards in a unique sort of comedy of Irish wit, gossip, satire, family quarrels, and family pride.

Chesterton then wrote about John B. Yeats:

> W. B. Yeats is perhaps the best talker I ever met, except his old father . . . Among twenty other qualities, he [John B. Yeats] had that very rare but very real thing, entirely spontaneous style . . . A long and elaborately balanced sentence, with dependent clauses alternative or antithetical, would flow out of such talkers with every word falling into its place, quite as immediately and innocently as most people would say it was a fine day or a funny business in the papers.

As the father continued to talk brilliantly and begin paintings and not finish them, as income from his Irish estate continued to dwindle and would end soon altogether when the Ashbourne Act of 1885 allowed tenants to buy the land outright from absentee landlords, Susan Pollexfen, in London, had a series of strokes and became a semi-invalid until her death on 3 January 1900.

Since she had believed she was marrying a man who was likely to become a prominent barrister or a judge, and since she disliked living in poverty in London, Yeats had reason to feel guilty about his failure to provide for his wife the life she had imagined. Twelve years after her death the remorse was still with him. He wrote to Lily: 'Had I had money your mother would never have been ill and would be alive now – *that is the thought always with me* – and I would have done anything to get it for her – but had not the art.'

In these years when he returned to London, John B. Yeats had neither the art nor the money. Although he had received a wind-fall from the sale of the land, it served mainly to pay off debts. While their father's financial circumstances worsened, all four of the Yeats children worked and made money. From early in their lives, they were serious, determined and industrious. By W. B. Yeats's thirtieth birthday, for example, as William Murphy wrote, he 'had published or made ready for publication seven books (and American editions of four of them), had seen 173 essays, letters, or poems published by 29 different periodicals, and had edited or contributed to 14 other volumes'. Both Lily and Lollie found work in design, embroidery and art teaching in London.

While neither of the girls married, Jack became an independent spirit as soon as he could, marrying at the age of twenty-three. William continued to live at home, in the family house in Bedford Park in London, even as he began to win fame as a poet and literary journalist and grew increasingly confident and eager to separate himself from his father.

It is interesting to watch him attack his father's friend Edward Dowden, when, at the age of twenty-one, he wrote an article for the *Dublin University Review*, as it is to watch him associate in London with others of his father's old literary friends, including John Todhunter, while excluding his father.

As W. B. Yeats interested himself in magic and the occult, his father, who had no time for such pursuits, was hostile. When Yeats the son received a letter from the old Fenian John O'Leary that

suggested that mystical pursuits would weaken him, he understood that the message had come from his father, responding:

> *The probable explanation . . . of your somewhat testy postcard is*
> *that you were out at Bedford Park and heard my father discoursing*
> *about my magical pursuits out of the immense depths of his*
> *ignorance as to everything that I am doing and thinking . . . The*
> *mystical life is the centre of all that I do and all that I write.*

When W. B. Yeats was thirty-one and his father fifty-seven, a
friend of the father wrote to a London editor suggesting that he
use some illustrations by John B. Yeats, 'a comparatively unknown
man', and introducing him as 'the father of Mr W. B. Yeats'.

While we have a lot of evidence of the growing fame of the
son, and the rifts and arguments, including threats of mild acts of
violence, between him and his father, we must also note that they
continued to live under the same roof and that many evenings
were ordinary and peaceful, and that they had many of the same
interests. In a brief diary that Lollie kept, for example, in 1888,
she noted that W. B. Yeats read aloud 'all evening' to his father.
Even when he left home, William was a regular visitor to Bedford
Park, especially when he was short of money.

It was clear that Yeats as a father could be not only exasperat-
ing but also inspirational. In 1910, W. B. Yeats, while preparing
lectures on drama, wrote to him: 'In the process of writing my
third lecture I found it led up to the thought of your letter which
I am going to quote at the end. It has made me realize with some
surprise how fully my philosophy of Life has been inherited from
you in all but its details and applications.' But eleven years later,
in a letter to John Quinn, he wrote about his father:

> *It is this infirmity of will which has prevented him from finishing*
> *his pictures and ruined his career. He even hates the sign of will*

> *in others . . . the qualities which I thought necessary to success in*
> *art or in life seemed to him 'egotism' or 'selfishness' or*
> *'brutality'. I had to escape this family drifting, innocent and*
> *helpless, and the need for that drew me to dominating men like*
> *Henley and Morris and estranged me from his friends . . .*

The father, in turn, was capable of finding his son irritating. In a letter to Lily in 1896, he wrote: 'Willie has been staying here the last few days. He has the greatest wish to be friendly and peaceable, but he can't manage it, and though I was very sorry to see him go, for he is in good humour, both most attractive and affectionate, still wherever he is there is constant strain and uneasiness.'

His irritation stretched from the son himself to the son's work. The following year, for example, he pronounced the play *The Shadowy Waters* as 'absolutely unintelligible'. In 1906, he wrote to Lady Gregory about his son's theories of drama: 'As to Willie's theories, there is not one of Shakespeare's dramas that does not reduce them to utter mockery.' And about his son's beliefs, in 1897, he wrote drily to the artist Sarah Purser: 'I don't know where Willie is or what he is doing. The last I heard was that he and [George] Russell had gone west (Sligo or thereabouts) to find a new God.'

He would also feel free to criticize his son's closest relationships, such as this from a letter to Lily written in New York in 1914: 'There could not be in the wide world two people more different from each other than Willie and Lady Gregory. Such a friendship or comradeship must be obstructive to the free play of natural feelings.' Despite his disapproval of his son's friendship with Lady Gregory, however, Yeats could use her as a vehicle to express annoyance with his son. When he heard about the poet's high-handed behaviour towards an actress at the Abbey Theatre, for example, he wrote to Lady Gregory to take the actress's side: 'I am sometimes tempted to say that if a man has the gift of words he is thereby unfitted for every position in life except that of writing.' In 1906, he wrote to Lady Gregory: 'Willie has a doctrinaire kind of mind. This is one of his difficulties, and makes a difficulty with his friends.'

These views did not stop him borrowing money from his son, writing to him, for example, early in 1902: 'Could you let Lily have a few pounds, as much as ten pounds or whatever you can?' And then in May: 'I am awfully sorry to ask you, but could you lend me two or even one pound – and could you send it by money order or postal order?' In 1904, when his son returned from a successful American tour, the father, whose requests for money from him had up to then been modest, asked him for a loan of twenty pounds (more than two thousand pounds in today's money). In that same year, when his son annoyed him, he wrote to Lily: 'I wish Willie had Jack's tender gracious manner, and did not sometimes treat me as if I was a black beetle.'

In 1901, Sarah Purser, indignant at how John B. Yeats had been treated by the Royal Hibernian Academy, mounted an exhibition in Dublin at her own expense of his work and that of the artist Nathaniel Hone. On the evening it opened, his son's play *Diarmuid and Grania*, written with George Moore, opened at the Gaiety Theatre in Dublin. And the following evening, an exhibition of paintings by Jack Yeats would open in Dublin too. The Yeatses were slowly starting to matter in Ireland.

In his catalogue note for Yeats's show, his friend York Powell wrote: 'A person, a thing, must appeal to his feeling, as well as to his intellect, before he can care enough about it to make it the subject of his brush . . . He will do but the thing he likes best, and he will only do the thing he likes.'

Sixty-three of his works were on display, including sketches and portraits. The reviews were good, as was attendance at the show. Soon afterwards, Yeats was contacted from New York by John Quinn, later to become his most serious patron and benefactor, who wanted to buy some portraits from him and to commission some others.

Despite the fact that he was becoming famous in Dublin, however, Yeats was broke once more, remaining in the city only because he did not have the fare to return to London. Gradually, however, without actually making a decision, he found himself settling in Dublin, to be followed in 1902 by his two daughters, who would be involved with Dun Emer, a design and printing workshop, to be followed eventually – in 1910 – by Jack and his wife, Cottie. W. B. Yeats was already spending a great deal of time in Dublin, taking part in setting up what would become the Abbey Theatre.

John B. Yeats's studio on St Stephen's Green became a place for people to stop by and talk. If often the conversation was more intense and polished than the work produced, the painter himself did not seem to mind. Among those who came to his studio was the English Jesuit Gerard Manley Hopkins, whose poems were not published until many years later, and among the regular visitors was John Millington Synge, whose work Yeats would defend vehemently.

Yeats even met the young James Joyce on the street. Joyce found him 'very loquacious'. When he painted the actor Frank Fay, Fay recorded: 'He was a peculiarly restless worker. He walked back and forward all the time, only halting now and again to use a tiny mirror from his pocket to see by reflection how the picture was getting on. Also he talked all the time, and it was the most entertaining talk I have ever listened to.' He also painted the lexicographer Father Dinneen, writing to John Quinn about the experience: 'It is not every day that a Protestant has a chance of buttonholing a priest, and I seized my chance to say what I am always wanting to say to Catholics.'

If Yeats liked someone, he made a sketch of them or even a portrait. He was not too bothered if they did not pay. Years later he wrote:

*I painted for nothing when I could not get the money. In Dublin money is not easy to be got. No one has any – but nice people with affectionate friends like to be painted . . . I have always said*

*that if I was dying and anyone came in and asked to be painted,*
*I could manage to put off the dying till the portrait was finished.*

His problem was that if he did not like someone, then he found it difficult to paint them. His work was an act of sympathy. 'I have always said of myself,' he wrote to John Quinn, 'that I can only paint *friendship portraits.*'

Yeats was also invited to stay at Coole Park by Lady Gregory, who wrote to John Quinn: 'I think him the most trying visitor possible in a house. Space and time mean nothing to him, he goes his own way, spoiling portraits as hopefully as he begins them, and always on the verge of a great future.' At Coole, he also left his socks lying about, but was neat, Lady Gregory noted, with his brushes, oils and palette.

Yeats could not be pinned down on any matter. In 1903, he wrote to his son: 'Admiration for English character is the greatest possible mistake. Its source is largely hunkering after the *fleshpots* of their beastly civilization.' Later in the year he wrote in Arthur Griffith's newspaper *United Irishman:* 'When their ill-gotten possessions are not molested or their right to universal thieving questioned, the English are a good-natured people, who steer the middle course, avoiding extremes; in matters of conduct, choosing compromise, and in matters of art, adoring the pretty. They have the lax morals and the easy manners of the genial highwayman and the footpad.'

Lollie Yeats, who ran the Dun Emer Press, later the Cuala Press, had considerable difficulties with her brother the poet, who wished to control what it published. Their father took the view that while William and Lollie had the morose and difficult manners of the Pollexfens, Lily and Jack had the lightness and charm that he associated with his own family. But he could change his mind about this too. In 1922, for example, he wrote to Lily: 'The Pollexfens all disliked Willie. In their eyes he was not only abnormal, but he seemed to take after me. But however irritable ("the crossest people I ever met," my sister Ellen called them) they were slothful and so let him alone. And therefore in Willie's eyes they appear something grand like the figures at Stonehenge seen by moonlight.'

During one row over the question of control at the Press, he wrote to his son, who had managed in a letter to insult all of his three siblings and infuriate Lollie. 'Why *do you write such offensive letters*? There is nothing fine in a haughty and arrogant temper. It is Fred Pollexfen's characteristic [Fred Pollexfen was an uncle of W. B. Yeats] and through it he got himself turned out of the family business . . . I think you ought to write a frank apology.' When his son did not apologize, his father wrote again: 'As you have dropped affection from the circle of your needs, have you also dropped love between man and woman? Is this your theory of the overman?'

He felt guilty that he was still not making enough money to pay for his own board, while his daughters went to work every day. He wrote to his son remorsefully: 'If only I could make a little success and a little money and help a little Dun Emer would be all right, and Lily and Lollie would be at ease. In a deeper sense than you will ever guess at, my want of success has made me the evil genius of the family.'

In *Ulysses*, as we have seen, Buck Mulligan gets to call Lily and Lollie Yeats 'the weird sisters' and 'two designing females'. Since their names were so alike, and they lived together and did the same kind of work, it is tempting to see them as interchangeable. But they were closer to warring factions and could not have been more different. Lily, the calmer one, and a great letter writer, had nothing good to say about her sister. Towards the end of Lily's life, when her sister was already dead, she wrote to a cousin:

*You were right about Lolly. She had very good brains and many talents but frittered them all away for want of balance. For the last twenty years I lived in dread of her losing her balance altogether. They were twenty years of Purgatory to me. It was curious that people writing after her death said how distinguished she looked and how much they admired her, but no one said they loved her.*

She also wrote: 'I hope in the next world I will be left with those of calm nerves and not egotists. I have had enough. I hope to be surrounded by calm, comfortable angels, and no fuss. Lolly probably hopes for a circus, organs, barrels, merry-go-rounds, not literally so, but racket round her and she in the middle on a pivot.'

William Butler Yeats, one of Lollie's main sparring partners, suggested that his sister had fallen out 'from the cradle' and told Lily: 'She is a tragedy, really never happy, always doing the wrong thing, restless, irritable, unloveable, unbalanced.' Despite the differences, the sisters were never apart. 'Lollie would go mad,' John B. Yeats wrote to a friend, 'if it were not for Lily, who is a haven of refuge and a harbour of peace, with whom she may weep her sad bosom empty.'

Living in the same house must have been wearing for Lollie, Lily and their father and not made any sweeter by the lack of difficulty with which the two Yeats brothers won fame and many admirers and managed to control their lives and their finances, keeping apart from the drama of the family when the notion took them and becoming involved when they were in the humour for it, William to cause trouble, Jack, as usual, to maintain his reputation for being lovable and unknowable in equal measure.

\*

By 1907, when John B. Yeats was sixty-eight, his high hopes for success as a painter in Dublin had come to nothing. People still visited his studio to talk rather than have their portrait painted. He arrived home every evening to war between his daughters. His son William became increasingly haughty and famous. And perhaps even worse, his son Jack, whom he barely saw as he was growing up, was industrious and determined and slowly becoming a successful painter and illustrator. And added to that, an Italian portrait painter of the very worst kind called Mancini had arrived in Dublin and was painting everybody. Even W. B. Yeats was using one of this Italian's portraits as a frontispiece to one of his books.

If, in 1907, news had spread that John B. Yeats was not long for the world, and, forlorn, was finally giving up the ghost, who would have been surprised?

His friends and supporters in Dublin raised money to lift his spirits by offering to send him to Italy, where he had never been. Lollie wrote to John Quinn: 'It is a splendid idea and most generous of them . . . I said the thing was to get Lily to get him to go . . . They just want him to see Italy and the great pictures and enjoy himself in his own way. It will be very hard to get him off.'

Soon, when he discovered that Lily was going to New York for an Irish Exhibition, Yeats decided that he would use the Italian money to accompany her. He bought a new suit and did two farewell pencil sketches of Edward Dowden before his departure. Since he kept his studio, his paints and brushes neatly stowed, and had plans for what he would do when he returned, it is unclear if he actually knew what he himself had in mind as he set out for New York. His moving back to Dublin from London had been done as drift rather than rational decision. So, too, with this.

On 21 December 1907, he sailed from Liverpool to New York. He would never return to Ireland, he would never see Lollie or Jack again, or his brother Isaac, or most of his old friends. And once Lily left him behind in America on her return to Dublin on 6 June 1908, he would never see her again either. 'My coming was a miracle of folly judged by human standards,' he wrote to Lily seven years later. 'I longed for someone to say to me that I should go away with you [back to Dublin]. But no one spoke, and it was again Providence that ordered the silence.'

John B. Yeats lived until his death in 1922 as a New Yorker, a much admired and loved figure in his adopted city. And since his family and friends were far away and he would need to write to them, he became one of the best letter writers of the age.

One of his son's major themes as a poet would be the vitality that remains in the spirit as the body ages. As W. B. Yeats did not now witness his father's slow and inevitable physical decline, but instead received many letters from the old man filled with good humour and wisdom and a soaring hunger for life and ideas, then his father's exile was enabling and inspiring for his son's work. And for his father, since he could not influence his son or mould his thinking in the day-to-day life of Dublin or London, exile was also a gift. He could attempt to influence W. B. Yeats and guide him, as he never had managed before, by writing to him intelligent and compelling letters about art and life, about poetry and religion, about his own hopes as an artist and his life in the city. Since the letters were so well written and original, his son would, at least some of the time, come to appreciate and admire his wayward and improvident father, just as he had kept him at a distance in London and Dublin.

In the meantime, with the help of John Quinn, the son would also have to provide for his father, pay the bills in the boarding house on West Twenty-Ninth Street, run by three Breton sisters called Petitpas, and ensure that he did not starve as, despite many pleas and cajolings, the old man refused to come home. Since John Quinn was a collector of literary manuscripts as well as paintings – he owned the manuscripts of *The Waste Land* and *Ulysses* as well as many Conrad manuscripts – he agreed to acquire W. B. Yeats's manuscripts and pay by covering his father's bed and board. He also commissioned sketches that he paid for in cash.

The letters John B. Yeats wrote to his son dealt with his reading and contained thoughts of astonishing freshness and seriousness on art and life, and on poetry. In April 1913, for example, he wrote to his son about the idea of newness:

*What is new is detestable to* poetry. *When we do like anything new it is when we recognize the old with a new gloss, as the dawn of a new day, or a young girl who is like her mother or her grandmother or her ancient mother Eve, or like to one's own sweetheart in some prenatal existence. I have just finished an article in which I maintain that art embodies not this or that feeling, but the whole totality – sensations, feelings, intuitions, everything – and that when everything within us is expressed there is peace and what is called beauty – the totality is personality. Now a most powerful and complex part of the personality is* affection *and affection* springs straight out of the memory. *For that reason what is new whether in the world of ideas or of fact cannot be subject for poetry, tho' you can be as rhetorical about it as you please – rhetoric expresses other people's feelings, poetry one's own.*

And on the notion of personality, he wrote:

*A man with a personality may talk about many things, but in things which touch his personality, he will prefer to be silent. Lincoln had this kind of silence, and Goethe when greatly moved became silent and wrote verses. Intellect and the moral sense can always explain themselves – they have words at command. Personality has too much to say for mortal speech. It can only exclaim – 'Here I am, look at me, and not with your corporeal eyes but with your spiritual eyes – with my imagery and my rhythm, and the loud music of my harp, I will rouse you from mortal sleep.'*

On Matthew Arnold's definition of poetry as 'criticism of life', Yeats wrote to his son that it was 'a bad heresy', managing a couple of aphorisms as he composed his letter: 'If the rose puzzled its mind over the question how it grew, it would not have been the miracle it is . . . The true poet is all the time a visionary and whether with friends or not, as much alone as a man on his death bed.'

The artist, he believed, should not admire life 'as does the American', although

> he occasionally by good chance may have admired some of it, he recoiled from most of it. If he was to live he must escape from the surface of life, and he found his asylum in his dreams; here was his workshop where he mended life . . . only in his dreams is a man really himself. Only for his dreams is a man responsible – his actions are what he must do. Actions are a bastard race to which a man has not given his full paternity.

In a later letter to his son, however, he emphasized the need for reality in the making of art: 'all art begins in portraiture . . . That is, a realistic thing identified with *realistic feeling*, after which and because of which comes the Edifice of Beauty – the great reaction.' Soon, however, he returned to the subject of dreams: 'The chief thing to know and never forget is that art is dreamland and that the moment a poet meddles with ethics and the moral uplift or thinking scientifically, he leaves dreamland, loses all music and ceases to be a poet.' Nonetheless, he needed to make clear to his son that believing dreams to be real was dangerous:

> The poet is a magician – his vocation to incessantly evoke dreams and do his work so well, because of natural gifts and acquired skill, that his dreams shall have a potency to defeat the actual at every point. Yet here is a curious thing, the poet and we his dupes know that they are only dreams – otherwise we lose them. With

*our eyes open, using our will and powers of selection, we,*
*together in friendship and brotherly love, create this dreamland.*
*Pronounce it to be actual life and you summon logic and*
*mechanical sense and reason and all the other powers of prose to*
*find yourself hailed back to the prison house and dreamland*
*vanishes – a shrieking ghost.*

Having sent his son this complex and urgent missive, which will strike any reader of W. B. Yeats's work as a fascinating effort to influence the work and change its direction, Yeats wrote to him again the following day, 22 December 1914, this time composing passages of great eloquence to invoke the power of art against that of science and thus send comfort to his son and, indeed, back to himself in his solitude and his weakness:

*Science exists that man may discover and control nature and build*
*up for himself habitations in which to live in ease and comfort.*
*Art exists that man cutting himself away from nature may build*
*in his free consciousness buildings vaster and more sumptuous*
*than these, furnished too with all manner of winding passages*
*and closets and boudoirs and encircled with gardens well shaded*
*and with everything that he can desire – and we build all out of*
*our spiritual pain – for if the bricks be not cemented and mortised*
*by actual suffering, they will not hold together. Those others live*
*on another plane where if there is less joy there is much less pain.*
*Like day labourers they work, with honest sweat to earn their*
*wages, and mother nature smiles on them and calls them her good*
*children who study her wishes and seek always to please her and*
*rewards them with many gifts. The artist has not the gift for this*
*assiduity, these servile labours – so falling out of favour with his*
*great mother he withdraws himself and lives in disgrace, and then*
*out of his pain and humiliation constructs for himself*
*habitations, and if she sweeps them away with a blow of her*

*hand he only builds them afresh, and as his joy is chiefly in the act
of building he does not mind how often he has to do it. The men
of science hate us and revile us, being angry with impotent rage
because we seem to them to live in profitless idleness, and though
we have sad faces we are yet of such invincible obstinacy that
nothing can induce us to join their ranks. There are other things
about us which perplex and offend them. They always work in
gangs, many minds engaged on one task, whereas we live and
work singly, each man building for himself accepting no
fellowship – for we say it is only thus we can build our
habitations. So it follows that they charge us with selfish egotism
and insolence and pride, and it is vain for us to say that we work
in the spirit of the utmost humility, not being strong enough for
their tasks, and suffering many pains because of the anger of our
offended and beloved mother. They are mighty men with strong
wills. We are weak as water, our weakness is our raison d'être,
and now and again when the strong man is broken he comes to us
that we may comfort him. We even may make merry together, for
we love our fellow men more than we do ourselves.*

He signed off: 'Yours affectionately – J. B. Yeats.'

A collection of passages from John B. Yeats's letters appeared
in a small book edited by Ezra Pound in 1917. Another small volume, edited by Lennox Robinson, appeared in 1920, with a
further small book edited by Pound in 1923. In 1944, Joseph Hone
selected a larger edition of the letters, published as *J. B. Yeats: Letters to His Son W. B. Yeats and Others*. This was reissued in an
abridged edition with an introduction by John McGahern in 1999.
But it was known in Dublin that an important cache of letters
remained in private hands. These were the letters written to Rosa
Butt, daughter of Isaac Butt, most of them during Yeats's exile in
New York.

The National Gallery in Dublin owns the tender and intriguing portrait Yeats painted of Rosa Butt in 1900, after his wife's death, when they were both sixty years of age or sixty-one. Rosa Butt has a distant dignity in the picture. Her face in repose has a fluidity as well as a stillness, a sadness but also the suggestion of a rich inner life, an aura in her gaze that has much that is withheld but also exudes a sense of comfort in the world. She is someone who looks as though she would enjoy company and also be content when alone. She has a freedom in her aspect that one could associate with what Yeats's son would call custom and ceremony, a freedom that gives her face and her pose in this picture a formidable and ambiguous power.

Since the painting was done in the year Yeats's wife died, it is easy to imagine the painter as an unsettled widower, whose life was funded mainly by his older son and controlled by his two unmarried daughters, and whose marriage had been less than happy, studying a woman whom he admired. All of his life he thought about what he might have become. That was one of his great subjects. He knew how much damage his impecunious ways had done to his wife and his daughters, but he knew also that, had he been a successful barrister, he would have ruined himself.

Now, after his wife's death, he had freedom and he chose further freedom. He chose to be bohemian and poor in Dublin and then in New York, to let his mind take him where it would, to seek out good company, to study life closely, to put more energy into his talk and his letters than into his art.

Rosa Butt appears in this portrait as a sensibility that he admired, but that would perhaps contain him. He did not wish to be contained. But there must have been times in the boarding house in New York when the poise in her face, the sense of ease and wit and civility that he gave her in this portrait, came to him as a dream of a life he did not have and recognized as oddly, sadly beyond him.

They agreed, as William Murphy noted in *Family Secrets*, to write to each other with total frankness and then each burn the other's letters as soon as they had been read. While Yeats kept his side of that bargain, Rosa Butt did not, although she may have destroyed a few letters that said too much. She saved just over two hundred of them. After her death in 1926, they passed into the keeping of her cousin, the painter Mary Swanzy, who eventually placed them in the Bodleian Library at Oxford with the strict proviso that they not be seen by anyone until 1979.

The final chapter of *Family Secrets*, 'John Butler Yeats and Rosa Butt', offers a summary of the letters and the relationship between the old painter in exile and the daughter of his father's friend. In the spring of 2017, I went back to the Special Collections at Union College in Schenectady to read the letters Yeats wrote to her.

By this time William M. Murphy was dead for almost a decade. He had lived until the age of ninety-two. His ghost had joined the other ones that haunted the halls of Union College, including the ghost of Henry James's father, who had briefly been a student here, and James's grandfather, who had helped to fund the college and whose portrait hung in the president's house.

Sometimes, as I wandered in the grounds and corridors, I was alert to the similarities between the two families – the Jameses and the Yeatses – and the similar ways in which two famous sons had been influenced by their father and in which they had handled his legacy.

In the autumn of 1828 when Henry James Senior, the father of the novelist, came to Union College, he entered fully into student life, drinking in taverns and having expensive suits made by the local tailor. He charged it all to his father, William, who was so wealthy that he owned the very land on which the campus of Union College was built. William James, who had been born in Bailieborough in County Cavan, was also one of the two trustees of the college.

Henry James Senior's departure from Union College, not long after his arrival, was the beginning of a journey in search of freedom of thought, eternal truth and interesting companions who were good listeners. James, like John B. Yeats, was a great talker. There are a number of other resemblances between the two men. Each of them, for example, married the sister of a classmate to whom they were close. Both of them suffered from, and also enjoyed, a lifelong indolence and restlessness; they dominated their households, but failed, or seemed to fail, in the larger world; they sought self-realization through art and general enquiry.

Both men created households where artists and writers visited and where becoming an artist was a natural development. Both men believed that the self was protean and they opposed both the settled life and the settled mind. Thus neither Henry James the novelist nor William Butler Yeats nor any of the Yeats siblings benefited from, nor had their minds destroyed by, a university education. Their fathers, believing themselves to be formidable institutions of higher learning in their own right, had little interest in exposing their sons to competition.

Both of the fathers were ambitious but often incapable of bringing a project to fruition. Talking for both took the place of doing, but both men were also capable of writing sentences of startling beauty.

Both men loved New York, not for its intellectual life but for its crowded street life, which they observed with fascination. Henry James Senior believed (or, to amuse a listener, claimed to believe) that the companionship of the crowded horse-car was the nearest thing to heaven on earth he had ever known. Their friends viewed both men as supremely delightful fellows; their company was much sought after. They both believed passionately in the future, seeing their children as fascinating manifestations of its power and possibility, at times much to their children's frustration.

They were both figures of real originality. On 4 June 1917, for example, some years before his son wrote his poem 'The Second Coming', John B. Yeats wrote to him: 'The millennium will come, and come it will, when Science and applied Science have released us from the burthens of industrial and other necessity. At present man would instantly deteriorate and sink to the condition of brutes if taken from under the yoke and discipline of toil and care.'

In a similar vein, Henry James Senior in 1879, almost two decades before his son wrote *The Turn of the Screw*, wrote the following account of a terror that came upon him on an ordinary evening in a rented house in Windsor Park:

> To all appearance it was a perfectly insane and abject terror, without ostensible cause, and only to be accounted for, to my perplexed imagination, by some damned shape squatting invisible to me within the precincts of the room, and raying out from his fetid personality influences fatal to life. The thing had not lasted ten seconds before I felt myself a wreck, that is, reduced from a state of firm, vigorous, joyful manhood to one of almost helpless infancy.

Each man had a daughter in possession of a rich and sharp and brittle intelligence, so brittle indeed that it would somehow prevent both Lily Yeats (and her sister, Lollie) and Alice James from separating from their families; both Lily and Alice had a magnificent and acid epistolary style.

Both fathers cared, it seemed, more about their elder children than the rest of their brood: William and Henry James and W. B. Yeats were treated differently than their younger siblings. John B. Yeats and Henry James Senior each fathered two genius sons, four men – Henry and William James, W. B. and Jack Yeats – who specialized, unlike their fathers, perhaps in spite of their fathers, in finishing almost everything they started. Three of them developed a complex, daring and extraordinary late style. All four boys studied art; William James had serious ambitions to be a painter. Two of them – W. B. Yeats and William James – began by dabbling in magic and mystical religion and went on to make it an important aspect of their life's work. While all four men were significantly influenced by their respective fathers – sometimes negatively – they had hardly anything to say about their respective mothers.

Both fathers used the Atlantic Ocean as a weapon in their arsenal, Yeats using it as a way of getting away from his family in old age, Henry James Senior using it as a way of further unsettling his unsettled children and indeed his loving wife.

Although Henry James the novelist saw a lot of Lady Gregory in London in the 1880s and 1890s, he was not a friend of W. B. Yeats. By the time Yeats had begun to flourish in London, James had withdrawn to Rye. James, however, attended a performance of Yeats's play *The Hour-glass* in Kensington in 1903, and in 1915 he contacted Yeats on behalf of Edith Wharton, asking for a poem for a fund-raising anthology for the war.

John B. Yeats had strong views on the question of Henry James. In July 1916 he wrote to his son: 'I have just finished a long novel by Henry James. Much of it made me think of the priest condemned for a long space to confess nuns. James has watched life from a distance.' When James's unfinished volume of autobiography was published posthumously in 1918, John B. Yeats wrote to a friend: 'Some believe that this war is a blessing disguised. It is enough for me that it stopped Henry James in writing a continuation of "The Middle Years".' Two years earlier, he wrote to William: 'Thinking about H James, I wonder why he is so obscure and why one's attention goes to sleep or wanders off when trying to make him out . . . In James, it is his cunning to make suspense dull, tiresome, holding you in spite of yourself.'

When an exasperated John Quinn wished to describe Yeats's endless and expensive stay in New York, he used James's late novel *The Ambassadors* as the example. 'The whole damn thing,' Quinn wrote, 'would make a perfect Henry James novel, and how he would get under your skin!' In this version of the story, Quinn made himself the Ambassador and Yeats the Lama:

*And so the book comes to a triumphant close with the victory of the Lama over his family, over the Ambassador, over the Doctor, over the nurse, and over his friends, it all being a triumphant vindication of the philosophy of the ego, of the victory of the man who regards only himself, of the man who does not care for others when they cease to amuse him, the artist's ego, the ego parading in the poet's singing robes, and – to use a vulgarism which Henry James would, I am sure, hugely enjoy – the egotist in his singing robes, crowned with laurel, the consummate artist, the playboy of West 29th Street, the youth of eighty without a care, with never a thought of his family or his friends, with eternal self-indulgence, with an appetite for food and drink at the age of eighty that is the envy of his younger friends and the despair of the Ambassador; this young man who has enjoyed fifty years of play and talk and health and high spirits and wine and drink and cigars, the man who enjoys the evasions of the artist – he 'gets away with it', as Henry James would say.*

In 1884, two years after the death of Henry James Senior, William, his eldest son, edited a selection of his writings. This publication caused Henry James the novelist to feel 'really that poor Father, struggling so alone all his life, and so destitute of every worldly or literary ambition, was yet a great writer'.

In 1922, when John B. Yeats died, John Quinn suggested that a new selection of his letters should be published. He wrote to W. B. Yeats: 'I feel very strongly that instead of making extracts from his letters, his letters should be published in full as were the letters of Henry James.' In this case, it was Henry James the son, who had died in 1916.

*

Rosa Butt lived in Battersea in London with her two sisters, Amy and Lizzie. Lizzie was a widow who specialized, it seemed, in disapproving of things. She had not taken any pleasure in her own marriage and she certainly took no pleasure in whatever was going on between her sister and Yeats. Her sister's disapproval of him was referred to in many of Yeats's letters to Rosa. He, in turn, disapproved of her sister's disapproval.

Even though their fathers had been lifelong friends, Yeats and Rosa Butt did not ever meet, it appears, until he was about twenty. 'When I first saw you,' he wrote to her years later, 'you were a woman grown (as well as growing) and I a hobbledehoy.' He thought her, he wrote, 'the most beautiful woman' he had ever seen. In the 1880s, when he visited her parents, he wrote, 'I used to listen to every word that concerned you.' It is clear that he saw her a number of times over the next ten years, and again in 1897, when York Powell remarked on her 'beautiful face'.

In the year before his wife's death, they began to correspond, the tone on his side affectionate. On 1 December 1900, when Susan Yeats was dead for almost a year, he wrote: 'You must not think I write to anyone as I write to you or *have ever done so.*' It is obvious that at some point in these next few years something happened between them. In the spring of 1906 when she was coming to Dublin, he wrote:

> *You must not* torture *me by treating me as if we were not*
> *something more, something much closer than lovers. In your*
> *letters you now treat me as I treat you, that is, as if there is*
> *between us an absolute intimacy. And you must do this when we*
> *meet . . . I feel myself to be yours* body and soul.

In a subsequent letter, he suggested marriage to her, even though they would both face problems – he had no money and she was timid and also felt an obligation to her sisters. After a single meeting with him on that visit to Dublin, she fled back to London.

Once he was installed in New York, Yeats began to write to her

about the relations between them not as something that might
have been, but rather as something alive and vivid, as though
they were young still and had all the time in the world and these
letters were part of a courtship. He seemed to enjoy writing
openly about his physical passion for her, knowing that she would
disapprove of his explicit tone. When he was seventy-one, for
example, he wrote:

> You are bright-eyed and alert, muscled and deliciously plump.
> You are so comely and so inviting, and so pleasant and plump in
> the places where you ought to be plump . . . If I were with you
> and we were alone I would coax you into good spirits. I would
> place my hand around your waist – one hand – and the other
> hand would distractedly find its way, however forbidden, into
> your bosom. And fighting with me would put you into good
> spirits and me into bad spirits.

The tone is affectionate, teasing, boyish, speculative. In 1908,
for example, he wrote: 'I often wonder if we had been man and
wife, [whether] I should have got on with you at all.' There is the
freedom in the letters of someone idly dreaming: 'I write to you
more freely and would talking [sic] to you more freely than anyone in the world. That is in my mind the relation between us.' He
confides in her the miseries of his marriage:

> I remember that my wife never failed to tell you bad news. If
> there was good news it did not seem to her worth talking about.
> It was only when things were going wrong that she spoke. It was
> the Pollexfen habit. They were a dour people. They trained each
> other so as to always keep their conversation and thoughts in the
> channels of the disagreeable. They were the most disagreeable
> people I ever met. All the time they were longing for affection . . .
> and their longing was like a deep unsunned well.

He wrote to her as a lover who had been accused of inconstancy:

*I am full of affection and longing for you and it is wrong of you to say I write to anyone as I write to you. To me you are always part and parcel of myself. I would as it were tell you things that I would not tell to myself. Can you understand this? – so that you are more to me than I am to myself.*

Or, six days later, as he worried about losing her to someone else: 'I got a dream which during its progress *much depressed me*. I dreamed that you were married, and that I asked why you had consented.'

The possibility of his going home remained a constant theme. In February 1908, he wrote: 'I don't know yet when I am returning . . . It is my last chance and if I don't make something of it I may go home for good.' The following month, he wrote: 'I don't know how I shall ever induce myself to leave New York.' In January 1909, he was still toying with the idea: 'I want to go home with a New York success behind me. I don't want to go home a failure, or even under suspicion of it. It is my last chance and I don't want to lose it.' Three days later, he wrote: 'I want it put on my tombstone that I was successful in America. Here lies J. B. Yeats much liked by his few friends and successful in America aged 98 years.'

Later in the year, he wrote: 'I must try another winter here. I cannot leave America *without a success, a real success*, and it is written on the cards. I am convinced that next week I shall succeed. The studio may be the beginning of a new epoch.'

Four months later, in November 1909, he noted that although Lily wanted him home for Christmas he would stay for a while longer: 'I won't go home till June. Ah! how I would love to have you in my room where no second bed would be wanted.' Three months later, he wrote: 'I think I may come home in May or June – certainly not April – and possibly July.'

This feeling that he would come home never left him, especially as each Christmas approached. In November 1915, he wrote: 'I shall return soon, I think.' But he also believed that New York had rescued him. In that same letter, he wrote: 'My time in Dublin was *awful*, and in London also. And I was never well. *New York saved my life.* That is God's truth.' Later that month he wrote: 'Why do I stay in New York when I expect every winter to be my last I don't know. I just stay on here, and dread Dublin as if it were a dark room haunted by a ghost.'

Intermittently, he was confident that he would be successful in New York, but often less sure about his relationship with Rosa, or at least the part of her that emerged in her letters:

> *To think of you is sometimes like crying for the moon. However, I shall return next spring, and with success and money, I hope, in which case I shall certainly see you, and if I have money* manage to see a great deal of you. *We have been never long enough together to have real confidences. That is why you don't give yourself away in your letters.*

He imagined her in the city with him: 'If you lived here in New York we should be sweethearts. Everyone would know it and everyone would respect the relation. No one would smile, offensively or inoffensively. They would think it natural and therefore right.' He imagined her as young: 'I have your secret and know you know that you are a young girl, as young as you ever were, and as capable of caresses – and of receiving them too sometimes.'

The problem of money persisted. On 20 January 1909, he wrote: 'My money here for lodgings and for board is long overdue and Mrs Ford [his first landlady] wrote to Quinn asking him to advise my return to Ireland.' And on 5 February, he reported that his debtors from Dublin were writing to him: 'With your letter came a *nasty* letter from a Dublin tailor. He writes as if I did not pay because I did not want to do so.'

When Quinn offered to pay his first-class passage back to Ireland, he wrote to Rosa: 'The bitterness of it is that I feel my reputation steadily rising.' He wanted to get a studio 'and paint all New York. Nothing will ever dislodge the idea from my mind I should go back sorrowful.'

When the summer came, his outlook grew sunny: 'You see I want an "old wife" . . . you want a husband to advise you. I won't call myself old, nor you either. In my thoughts you are young as ever.'

But eleven days later, he was less sure of her:

*In the most abominable way you keep me at a safe distance. I have always felt it, though till now I have never complained of it. Of course it is that you do not trust me, and this I know cannot be cured unless I went to London and stayed there long enough for the feeling of intimacy to be created, this mysterious intimacy that I am always trying to create at a single stroke, but which you will have on no terms.*

He wrote about how much he admired America: 'The good thing about a Democracy is that it can correct its errors and repent of its misdeeds.' And how much he admired New York: 'I love the people here, and so would you, *after a while*. At first your conservative instincts would be shocked, but in a little you would cease to struggle and go with the stream.'

In a number of letters they argued, as most people in their world did, about the personality of George Moore:

*I know you like to hear of people but I find it increasingly difficult to write to you about people, as with your early Victorian psychology you always misunderstand people . . . As to Moore, you have made up your mind long ago, so it is needless to*

*talk any further. To make up your mind in an instant and stick
to it all your life is a feminine characteristic of the early
Victorian mind. How well I remember it . . . This is Victorian
psychology to think no evil of your friends and all evil of
everyone outside your friends. I think my tendency is exactly the
other way around . . . I don't like George Moore because he is
obscene in a callous sort of way, but I like his way of seeking his
own pleasure. That is why he is always interesting and
refreshing, and one feels a sort of gravitation to him for being so.*

Sometimes his letters were filled with tenderness, at other
times the tone was tough. In November 1909, for example, he
wrote: 'As to your father, I never doubted your love . . . but I still
think you hate all his political ideas, to which he gave his life and
his genius.' And also: 'Having to live among stupid people, you
have adopted all their stupid imbecilic ideas, and deserted
your father's noble political ideas.' But two months earlier, he
had written:

*I think of you constantly again and again, put myself to sleep
thinking of you, fancying myself married to you, and both of us
young, picturing to myself what you would say and do and what
we would say to each other . . . I love you every way. I think I
love you best when you are cross.*

And having enclosed a sketch, he wrote:

*Here you are as I think of you when I fancy myself married to
you. You look a little timid. You are just entering the bridal
chamber . . . How nice you look, the big crinoline and the white
drawers peeping underneath and the wide-eyed seriousness . . . I
wish so much you would never doubt yourself, or your
power over me.*

And two months later: 'You are a prude, although your heart is as hot as a coal of fire.'

Some of his letters dealt with their little arguments:

*I have always known you to have intellect and to be your father's daughter . . . and I try to make my letters intellectual, thinking to interest you, and yet you always treat me as if I was insulting you, which is early Victorian with a vengeance. I sometimes try to make them amusing and there also I fail.*

Two months later: 'You in Dublin among the people you like and who like you but make you hard-hearted towards everything I like, so that I am afraid that I might say something in my letter that may be quite out of tune with your ideas.'

Whatever had happened between them in Dublin when they had been alone in his studio continued to interest him: 'I am always so glad you think about the studio. I am always thinking of it, and I *know we both love to think of it,*' he wrote in February 1910. And then the following month: 'I wish you *would* try and *shock* me . . . I once had a chance with you and my courage failed, but if ever again I get a chance my courage won't fail.' And five days later: 'Merely to think and dream of kissing you throws all my senses into delirium, like a thirsty man who sees a vision of a lake.' And then the following month: 'There are so many things I want to say to you, things that could only be *spoken* and that I think would only be said between a man and a woman in the sort of intimacy that arises between a man and a woman who love and trust each other.'

In May 1910, having written: 'You are a kettle with the lid open. I . . . am a kettle with the lid shut,' he began to dream about the life they could have had:

*It is a pity that you and I did not live together, your quick mind and my slow one . . . I would have taught you philosophy, for which I have*

*a talent and you none, and you would have taught me concrete*
*visible life in all its poetical and humorous details. We would have*
*been great friends and lovers. What nice little admonitions you would*
*have whispered to me from your pillow as we lay together talking far*
*into the night. But this is dangerous ground which I must avoid.*

And a few months later:

*Some time ago Quinn asked me did I ever strip an amorous*
*woman. I answered with a loud 'No, never.' 'Ah,' he said, 'you*
*have missed a great pleasure!' . . . Your bosom is as soft and*
*round as when you were eighteen, and your spirit, your inner*
*self, is like your bosom.*

And again in October: 'I love you. I can't tell you why. I dreamed of
you last night, saw you sitting handsomely dressed, with your
ankles showing, and the drawers quite visible . . . So perhaps you
see *how* I love you.' And in a postscript: 'I often think of making lots
of pictures for your eye, you and I married and young in our
bedroom standing together looking at ourselves in the looking
glass on the first night and before anything has happened, and
then our picture *after*. Ah! Rosa, Rosa, it makes me tremble to think
of you.'

This ebullient and teasing tone was tempered in other letters
as the real world impinged. The previous June he had written
starkly: 'None of my projects have materialized. Some failed
utterly.' And now in October 1910, as there was a possibility that
his son would be made a professor at Trinity College: 'I think if
Willie is made a Professor and Lily and Lollie are better off all my
resolution will break down and I will go home.' As Christmas
approached, he began to miss Dublin: 'I am terribly homesick,
only the more I long for home the more I feel its hopelessness.
Here my work lies but my affections are in Ireland, especially

now, for I always enjoyed Xmas at home, since Lily and the others are naturally festive and rise to these occasions.' The following day he wrote again: 'I am longing to be at home, but the more I long the keener is my sense of its impossibility.' And a month later, as Christmas was close, he wrote: 'I am horribly homesick.'

The following year he was still thinking about success: 'It would be a cruel thing if, just as I had made all my preparations for returning, offers of work etc should pour in *forcing* me to stay. I have slaved all my life for success, so if success [were] offered I could not refuse it.'

And again there was always the problem of money. On 27 January 1911, he wrote to Rosa: 'I am frightfully behindhand with my money and so have a horrible *haunted* feeling night and day.' More than two years later, in April 1913, he wrote: 'Yesterday, had it been possible I would have taken the first steamer home.' In November 1914, he wrote: 'I can tell you that I am sometimes so worried that I have to walk the streets to keep my nerves quiet.'

Exile gave Yeats a chance to think about his family and his wife's family. In October 1910, he wrote to Rosa: 'One reason why I am so incensed against class distinctions is because those very small gentry around Sligo always excluded the Pollexfens from their friendship.' And a month later: 'The Pollexfen family hated personal feeling, nothing for them but *rules*, the dour mind, hard, unfeeling, but honest.' And in April 1913: 'My wife's relations thought it an indecency to be cheerful. I think that to show sorrow is an indecency.' He also wrote about the connection between his daughter Lollie, who was visiting Rosa, and her mother:

> Lollie will be with you now, a curious little creature who has two demons. As a Yeats, she is gay and affectionate, looking on the best side of things. As a Pollexfen, she has a tendency to be gloomy and pessimistic, with a desire to wound her best friends, to positively stab them to the heart, though only so as words go. The last

*characteristic she inherits directly from her mother . . . When the*
*fire has passed, she does not remember having said anything that*
*could hurt anyone's feelings. This also was a trait of her mother's.*

He continued to let Rosa know that he loved her and that he imagined how they would be were they together: 'You don't know how I love you, reasonably,' he wrote in September 1912, 'but above all unreasonably, and you would have me all reason.' And then a month later: 'Had we married, you would be all for movement, and I for sitting still, and we should have fought like cat and dog, and everyone would have sympathized with you and called me a pig, and I'd have called myself a lazy pig.' And two days later: 'If you and I were together and by ourselves I would give you such a loving embrace that all youth would start up in your veins. Ah, I won't say what thoughts are in my head *and in my veins.*' And a month later: 'I am longing to spend some hours with you, though I never let my mind dwell on the subject. It is too painful and too tantalizing. I don't even like you to allude to it *for it can't be helped.* It only disturbs us both.'

Early the following year, Yeats grew more explicit: 'Had we married, I'd have enjoyed sometimes making you angry, say the last thing at night your eyebrows black and horizontal, and you standing in your nightgown – and I longing for you. That's how we would play the game and you would know perfectly well that the front of your nightgown was open.'

In this correspondence that centred on impossible or dreamed-of love and the imagined loved one, it is easy to think of W. B. Yeats's long and impossible attachment to Maud Gonne, or, since this is a story of love in old age, Yeats's early poem that began:

> When you are old and grey and full of sleep,
> And nodding by the fire, take down this book,

> And slowly read, and dream of the soft look
> Your eyes had once, and of their shadows deep.

But these letters to Rosa Butt are not letters of regret about a lost love, or a love not reciprocated, or written with sadness now that the years have passed. Rather, they are filled with defiance in the face of old age. Thus they are closer to some poems about age that W. B. Yeats wrote after his father's death. For example, lines such as these from 'The Tower':

> Never had I more
> Excited, passionate, fantastical
> Imagination, nor an ear and eye
> That more expected the impossible . . .

Or lines from 'The Wild Old Wicked Man' such as:

> 'Because I am mad about women
> I am mad about the hills,'
> Said that wild old wicked man
> Who travels where God wills . . .

Or:

> 'A young man in the dark am I,
> But a wild old man in the light . . .'

Or:

> 'But a coarse old man am I,
> I choose the second-best,
> I forget it all awhile
> Upon a woman's breast.'

Or Yeats's late poem 'The Apparitions', which includes the lines:

> When a man grows old his joy
> Grows more deep day after day,
> His empty heart is full at length,
> But he has need of all that strength
> Because of the increasing Night
> That opens her mystery and fright.

Or the last stanza of 'Are You Content':

> Infirm and aged I might stay
> In some good company,
> I who have always hated work,
> Smiling at the sea,
> Or demonstrate in my own life
> What Robert Browning meant
> By an old hunter talking with Gods;
> But I am not content.

Or his short poem 'The Spur':

> You think it horrible that lust and rage
> Should dance attendance upon my old age;
> They were not such a plague when I was young;
> What else have I to spur me into song?

Or the lines in 'An Acre of Grass':

> Grant me an old man's frenzy,
> Myself must I remake
> Till I am Timon and Lear . . .

Or the last stanza of 'A Prayer for Old Age':

> I pray – for fashion's word is out
> And prayer comes round again –
> That I may seem, though I die old,
> A foolish, passionate man.

In these letters to Rosa Butt, John B. Yeats, the foolish, passionate man, with his excited, passionate, fantastical imagination, did not write about the life he had missed, but the life he imagined, and he gave that life a sense of lived reality, as though it were not only somehow possible, but almost present. In January 1914, for example, he made clear that he saw their correspondence as a sort of marriage:

> *One of the charms of marriage is that two people can talk to each other of things that the woman would not talk of to other women or the man to other men, and that is why I insisted on our letters being burned, so that you and I could write to each other as if in married frankness, and I do write to you as if you were my real wife and one flesh with me (which also you are not in reality).*

And in an earlier letter, he wrote about their marriage as though they were living it in slow detail, having arguments in real time:

> *All my life I have longed for the friendship of a clever woman, but you will give almost anything except your intellect . . . Had we married years ago, we should have fought the question, only sometimes together late at night, my arms around your waist, my dear, you cross and I coaxing, perhaps burying your face in the pillow to escape my kissing you – gradually you would have got quiet and at least passive, and in the morning as you went about the room dressing I would have stolen furtive glances at you to see*

*how you were taking it. And at breakfast we would have been a*
*little formal, your face fixed, and if I stroked your hand you*
*would have pulled it away. Perhaps I would have stroked your*
*breast, and you would have moved, as if to let me know that it*
*was nothing to you what I did, and I'd have felt bad all day, and*
*so would you. After a few days, we'd both get hungry for each*
*other, but neither would give in. But for want of courage, you*
*would think of asking for a separate room, not that you really*
*meant it, but just as a demonstration. Suddenly some[thing]*
*moving, something very delightful would happen, perhaps one of*
*the children would show itself particularly nice and good (and all*
*our children would have been nice, affectionate at any rate) . . .*

While we get so much of John B. Yeats, all we have of the
recipient of these letters is a photograph of her, a pencil sketch
by Yeats and his portrait of her. Since Yeats burned Rosa's letters,
we do not have her voice except for four words that he repeats in
an undated letter. The four words are 'My dear old lover'. And
they suggest that her side of the correspondence was, in its own
way, ardent, even if not as open and honest as his side. ('You think
the correct thing for a woman, when she writes a letter, is to say
nothing and do it over a long letter.') Despite the fact that we
only have this single phrase, what is strange is how vividly Rosa
emerges in these letters from him to her. For example, it is clear
that she does not share in his easy lewdness. ('Not for worlds
would you write these words: "bottom" or "thigh", nor would
you allude to your breasts.') And there was nothing impetuous
about her. She does not write to say that she is coming to New
York on the next steamer or that he must return to Dublin or
London forthwith and marry her.

As he writes not only about how he feels about her, but with
news about his life, where he has been and who he has met, with
much gossip about John Quinn, and reference to 'free love' in

America, with confessions about how he once and only once strayed during his years of marriage to Susan Pollexfen, she writes back to him time and again, and as she does so we feel, from ways in which he responds, her kindness, her reticence and her calm intelligence and stability.

The idea that she kept the letters also matters. She knew of their value. What Yeats wrote, in all its honesty and wild impracticality and open sexuality, may have brightened up her life, but in the care he took with his letters to her and the amount of sweet emotion in them, there is a sense that her life was more than worthy of such brightening, that she was a rare spirit who did as much justice as she could to her correspondent, who responded to her 'My dear old lover' with: 'And we are lovers. And if we meet and when we meet, we shall kiss and be young and then kiss, our bodies and souls meet.'

As they grew further into their seventies, he worried about himself and about Rosa. In April 1913, when he was seventy-four, he wrote: 'I know of course that the sands are running low and that presently I shall begin to notice that my memory is beginning to fade.' And in October: 'All last night I had vivid and broken dreams about you. I cannot remember them except that they were very miserable. I often woke and then bitterly reproached myself that I had not for a moment anticipated that you *could be sick*.' In January 1915, he wrote: 'At my age months count as much as they do when we are children.'

But always he would recover from his melancholy and return to his old self again: 'Do you think I would have fallen in love with you if there was not plenty of Venus? It was Venus herself that decorated you with the breasts in which I take such delight.' Two months later, he wrote to her again about her breasts: 'I would like to make a portrait of them with the little pink nipples.'

And then a month later, he wrote once more about what would have happened had they married:

*Alas! that we did not marry! You would have made a man of me,
and I would have made you the woman that you are and that
you do not know you are . . . I often in imagination look back
and see you with my baby at your breast, both of us watching it,
and yet – and yet – I think that perhaps our children would have
been unhappy, at any rate living in Britain.*

He worried sometimes that he was losing her. In May 1914, he
wrote: 'Is it my fault or is it yours that you have lost interest in me
and my letters?' The following month, he wrote:

*Had we married and lived together, our mutual unlikeness would
have made us perfectly interesting to each other. I fancy you love
Religion while I hate it, because of all its sins and wickedness. I
am a radical socialist anarchist Home Ruler, everything you
abhor, so I sometimes think it would be best to let this
correspondence drop. If I go home this year we shall meet and
have many talks and then start again to write to each other.*

And again in October he questioned the point of their correspondence, becoming almost rude to her: 'But you can be dull
beyond words, and you give me no thanks for my efforts to write
amusing letters . . . I am disposed to think and believe that I bore
you to death and the correspondence is only a bother to you.'

Although Rosa Butt's father, as we have seen, had been the one
to place the words 'Home Rule' at the centre of the debate between
Ireland and England, Rosa herself was, it seems, not a Home Ruler.
As the political atmosphere in Ireland heated up in the second
decade of the twentieth century, Yeats had much to say to her
about politics and changing life in Dublin. In January 1913, he
wrote: 'Ireland is progressing, beginning to take an interest in intelligent things, in poetry and art, but all this is to you nothing. You are

about as interested in ideas as if you were a nun, or a priest, or a Swanzy.' (Rosa Butt's mother was a member of the Swanzy family.)

The following year, he wrote: 'Were he [her father] a young man and growing up, how happy he would be! – for Dublin is in the grip of the young poets – how happy and free!' In January 1916, he wrote about Ireland again: 'I have always said that I am for Home Rule in order to rescue Irish Protestants from greed and vulgarity, but though you are Isaac Butt's daughter, there is no use talking to you about Home Rule – alas! I think Irish Protestants are the meanest people on earth and have always thought so.'

In the immediate aftermath of the 1916 Rebellion, on the very day of Patrick Pearse's execution for his part in the uprising, he wrote to her: 'It was a folly but a heroic folly.' And two months later: 'These events in Ireland because of the executions are now the most important and the most blessed in Irish history. You don't know how often I wished for your father. What he needed all his life was a great crisis, which while leaving everyone else bewildered would have found in him the statesman.' In January 1917, he wrote to her an astute comment about the American response to the Rebellion: 'The execution of the fifteen by Sir J. Maxwell seems to Americans something so *out of date*, and to be out of date is a crime in America. Ireland stands very high with every one. Her repute grows daily.'

And the following day he wrote again with more news about Ireland: 'A wonderful Irish novel has just appeared, called "A Portrait of the Artist as a Young Man" by Joyce.'

In 1916 and 1917, it is obvious that his letters were not receiving a sufficient response from her. But his tone remained fond, if often hectoring. 'I wish you and I had a talk. I am always in vision seeing you and me sitting together under a shading tree in your park while I tell you some of what I hear in America and I hear your mocking and humorous laughter.' And in an undated letter from the same period: 'I can't understand why all your life you have put up with so many tiresome people.' And also: 'I wish I had married

[you] years ago. Had I done so you would now be more cheerful, or I would have become as low-spirited as you are. I think I could have rescued you from some of your depressing friends.'

In stray comments, he disparaged Rosa's sister Lizzie and blamed her on one occasion for Rosa's failure to write. When Lizzie became ill, we catch a glimpse of Yeats at his most impossible when he suggested to Rosa that she send her sister away: 'Among strangers she would be perfectly well. Invalids of her kind should be kept among strangers.' This reminded him of his daughter and his wife:

*She [Lollie] gets [along] perfectly well among strangers, as long as they remain strangers. If she knew them too well, she hates them. Lollie's mother was the same . . . I used to wonder what was the matter with her and why she hated so many people and said such vitriolic things . . . At first when Susan insulted me and my friends I used to mind a great deal, but afterwards I did not mind at all. She was perfectly convinced that she herself was always right and everybody else was wrong.*

A month later, he made clear how much he wanted Rosa's praise, as though he himself were the subject of his son's poem 'Her Praise', which would appear in the volume *The Wild Swans at Coole* in 1919, and began: 'She is foremost of those that I would hear praised': 'I don't think you have studied my character. I like to be praised, and I would rather be praised by you than by anyone else in this world. Yet you never praise me.'

But no matter what he wanted from Rosa Butt, the memories of his marriage continued to haunt him:

*I became engaged on two or three days' acquaintance, and it was not from first love or love at all (this really* entre nous *– I have never confessed it to anyone) but just destiny. The Pollexfen family revolted me and at the same time greatly attracted me,*

*and have never lost that attraction . . . I used to enjoy hearing my
poor wife talk of other people. She was always wrong, but her
mistakes were more interesting than other people's right
judgement.*

And on Christmas Eve 1918, he wrote: 'My poor dear wife had no
luck.'

Despite his constant talk about it, he still had not finished the
self-portrait. On Christmas Eve 1918 he also wrote:

*My programme at present is to finish the portrait of myself for
Quinn, then write a lot more memoirs, and finish an article for
the North American Review, and then* come home – *to my
sweetheart and my family . . . My portrait looks well. One day
since my illness (the day before yesterday) I almost finished the
hands and put a life and authority in it such as I have never
reached any time before.*

It surely did not escape Rosa Butt's attention that he had now
been working on the self-portrait for seven years and that the
idea of his coming home to his sweetheart had to be tempered
not only with the knowledge that such previous promises had
come to nothing, but also with the fact that they were both
almost eighty years old.

As pressure from his children and from Quinn mounted on
him to return to Dublin, he wrote on 9 March 1919, a week before
his eightieth birthday: 'Had I stayed in Dublin I should have died
years ago . . . Coming here saved my life. I have been afraid to go
back.' When John Quinn offered to pay for a nurse to accompany
him, he wrote: 'I told him I would as soon travel with an orang-
utang.' In March the following year, after a visit from his son and
daughter-in-law, he wrote: 'I told Willie and George that if I went

home I would have to bid farewell to painting and be just an old man in his second childhood.'

In November, he wrote: 'The people at home are making great effort to bring me home.' And the following March, two days after his eighty-second birthday: 'Willie finds that he cannot keep me here.' Then in November: 'I propose sailing Dec 3rd but may stay longer . . . Some unknown rich person through a friend has offered to finance me if I wish it, and I may accept the generosity. The portrait is my magnum opus, and I can't desert it.'

As he came to the end of his life, the old painter still imagined what could have been: 'Had we married I would have had a great struggle with you and never rested till I had won your confidence.' And the following month: 'I shudder when I look back over my life. It would not have been so bad had you been with me.' When he heard that Rosa's sister Amy had died, he wrote: 'A thin wall divides all of us from the abyss of despair. Not to break through this slender partition is the whole struggle of my life for if I get but one glimpse into that abyss my whole efficiency and power of work is gone for the day.' The following month, he wrote again about how much he imagined being with Rosa: 'You are lonely and sad and I suppose old. I wish I was near you. We should see each other every day. When we found ourselves alone we should exchange kisses . . . I remember perfectly what it tastes [sic] to kiss you.'

As his son's fame continued to grow, and his own work seemed to have come to nothing, John B. Yeats was given further reason to shudder when in 1921, the last year of his life, W. B. Yeats wrote a short section of autobiography called 'Four Years', serialized in *The Dial* and later published in book form by Cuala Press, overseen by Lollie. The four years in question were years of poverty in London, when Yeats the poet was still living in his father's house. Roy Foster in his biography of the poet wrote:

And in the portrait of JBY was etched all his negligence, improvidence, and superb carelessness – as well as the alarm he aroused in his children. The unhappiness which pervades the book could be read as an indictment of the world created (or unmade) by the author's father, even if the implicit message was that insecurity acted as the nursery of genius.

In the book, W. B. Yeats described returning from Oxford during that period to his 'enraged family'. The implication was that they were enraged by his father's indolence and inadequacies.

His father wrote to him:

*Why 'enraged family'? I remember when you came back from Oxford how glad I was to see you and hear your account of your visit . . . As to Lily and Lollie, they were too busy to be 'enraged' about anything, Lily working all day at the Morrises and Lollie dashing about giving lectures on picture painting and earning close on three hundred pounds a year . . . while both gave all their earnings to the house. And besides all this work, of course, they did the housekeeping and had to contrive things and see to things for their invalid mother . . . They paid the penalty of having a father who did not earn enough . . . I am sure that 'enraged family' was a slip of the pen.*

To Lollie, he wrote: 'We must submit and pay the penalty for knowing a poet . . . I am quite sure Willie has no malice against us, but just wants to tell histories . . . I don't really now complain of his contempt, but it should not be revived in his book for the benefit of his glory.'

The next day, with all this on his mind, he composed his most eloquent attack on his son's work and sent it to him:

*When is your poetry at its best? I challenge all the critics if it is not when its wild spirit of your imagination is wedded to concrete fact. Had you stayed with me and not left me for Lady Gregory, and her friends and associations, you would have loved and adored concrete life for which I know you have a real affection. What would have resulted? Realistic and poetical plays – poetry in closest and most intimate union with the positive realities and complexities of life. And that is the world that waits, so far in vain, for its poet.*

He went on:

*Am I talking wildly? Am I senile? I don't think so, for I would have said the same any time these 20 or 30 years. The best thing in life is the game of life, and some day a poet will find this out. I hope you will be that poet. It is easier to write poetry that is far away from life, but it is* infinitely *more exciting to write the poetry of life – and it is what the whole world is crying out for as pants the hart for the water brook. I bet it is what your wife wants – ask her. She will know what I mean and drive it home. I have great confidence in her. Does she have the courage to say it? Had you stayed with me, we would have collaborated and York Powell would have helped. We should have loved the opportunity of a poet among us to handle the concrete which is now left in the hands of the humorists and the preachers.*

As William M. Murphy wrote in his biography: 'Willie received the resentments as a Pollexfen. When he returned the Cuala proofs to Lollie, he suggested that she change the word "enraged" to "troubled", but added, "Do not make it if it upsets the type too much." It was all very well to mollify the old man if no inconvenience were involved, but not otherwise. He refused to pursue the matter further with his father.'

John B. Yeats died in his sleep on 3 February 1922. W. B. Yeats wrote to Lily:

*If he had come home he would have lived longer but he might have grown infirm, grown to feel himself a useless old man. He has died as the Antarctic explorers died, in the midst of his work & the middle of his thought, convinced that he was about to paint as never before . . . Several times lately (the last, two or 3 months ago) he wrote of dreaming of our mother . . . I think in spite of his misfortunes that his life has been happy, especially of recent years; for more than any man I have ever known he could live in the happiness of the passing moment.*

*The Two Tenors: James Joyce*
*and His Father*

In his book *Yeats: The Man and the Masks*, Richard Ellmann quotes Ivan Karamazov: 'Who doesn't desire his father's death?' Ellmann wrote:

> From the Urals to Donegal the theme recurs, in Turgenev, in Samuel Butler, in Gosse. It is especially prominent in Ireland. George Moore, in his *Confessions of a Young Man*, blatantly proclaims his sense of liberation and relief when his father died. Synge makes an attempted parricide the theme of his *The Playboy of the Western World*; James Joyce describes in *Ulysses* how Stephen Dedalus, disowning his own parent, searches for another father . . . Yeats, after handling the subject in an unpublished play written in 1884, returns to it in 1892 in a poem 'The Death of Cuchulain', turns the same story into a play in 1903, makes two translations of *Oedipus Rex*, the first in 1912, the second in 1927, and writes another play involving parricide, *Purgatory*, shortly before his death.

In his work, James Joyce sought to recreate his father, reimagine him, fully invoke him, live in his world, while at the same time making sure that, from the age of twenty-two, with the exception of a few short visits to Dublin, he did not see him much. Since his father's presence loomed so large in his Dublin, he would go into exile not only to escape the city of his birth but so that both Dublin and the man who had begotten him could move into shadow.

Just as Oscar Wilde began to become himself in the very year after his father's death, and John B. Yeats managed, figuratively, to kill his son by going into exile, so too James Joyce managed to kill his father by leaving him to his fate in Dublin, seeking, in his father's absence, not only to forge the uncreated conscience of his race but to find shape for the experience of his father, to resurrect him, to offer life to what had become shadow.

In this world of sons then, fathers become ghosts and shadows and fictions. They live in memories and letters, becoming more complex, fulfilling their sons' needs as artists, standing out of the way. As Stephen Dedalus in *Ulysses* says: 'A father . . . is a necessary evil.' And later in the same speech: 'Paternity may be a legal fiction. Who is the father of any son that any son should love him or he any son?'

But Joyce's relationship to his father was more complex than either Wilde's or Yeats's. In *My Brother's Keeper*, Stanislaus Joyce muses on his brother's relationship to his parents: 'Every man who has known the torment of thought attaches himself spiritually to one or the other of his parents . . . in the case of an author the elective affinity strongly influences his artistic production.' In the case of his brother, he wrote, the attachment was to his father.

Stanislaus Joyce makes a distinction between literature and life:

> In *Ulysses* Simon Dedalus, for whom my father served as model, is a battered wreck in whom even the wish to live carefree has become a vague memory, but if the facets of his character that are presented make the figure an effective and amusing literary creation, that is possibly only because the tolerance of literature greatly exceeds that of actual life.

John Stanislaus Joyce was born in Cork in 1849. Like his father and his grandfather, he was an only son. The family were well-to-do merchants and property owners, prominent in local politics. As a youth, in order to build up his health, John Stanislaus's father found him work on the pilot boats that operated in Cork Harbour. As his son, Stanislaus, later wrote, he was allowed to

> go out on the pilot boats that went to meet the transatlantic liners, for which in those days Queenstown was a port of call . . . Besides the robust health which he acquired from the briny Atlantic breezes he learned from the Queenstown pilots the varied and fluent vocabulary of abuse that in later years was the delight of his bar room cronies.

When he was eighteen, a year after his father's death, John Stanislaus went to Queen's College in Cork to study medicine. While he did not finish his degree, he enjoyed himself enormously as a student, having a fine tenor voice and becoming involved in amateur theatre. Having left college, he began working as an accountant in Cork before moving to Dublin with his mother at the age of twenty-four to work as secretary in a distillery in which he had bought shares situated in Chapelizod on the banks of the Liffey.

John Stanislaus was a popular fellow and much admired for his singing. Stanislaus reported that on his last evening in Cork at a gala dinner in his honour a leading English tenor 'said he would willingly have given two hundred pounds there and then to be able to sing that aria as my father had sung it'. In Dublin he sang at concerts and attended many recitals, where he heard the great singers of the age.

When, a few years after his arrival in Dublin, the distillery at Chapelizod went into liquidation, thus causing Joyce to lose his job and most of the £500 – over £50,000 in today's money – that he had invested in the company, he began to work as an accountant again. He walked the city looking for business, doing the accounts of small firms or becoming involved in liquidations.

Soon he became secretary of the United Liberal Club, which

welcomed both Liberals and Home Rulers in a time when Isaac Butt's leadership of the Irish Parliamentary Party was giving way to that of Charles Stewart Parnell. The Club in Dawson Street was a place to meet and smoke and drink and discuss politics.

Joyce played an active part in the elections to the Westminster Parliament in 1880. In the Dublin constituency where he worked, the two Conservative candidates – including Sir Arthur Guinness – were defeated and a Liberal and a Home Ruler elected. For his tireless efforts on the campaign, John Stanislaus was given a bonus as part of the celebrations.

As this campaign was going on, Joyce got to know May Murray, who was then nineteen. She had been trained to sing and play the piano by her aunts, who were well known in musical circles in Dublin. May's father disapproved of Joyce, as Joyce's mother disapproved of May. The two were living close to each other in Clanbrassil Street, near where James Joyce would later have Leopold Bloom in *Ulysses* spend his childhood. When it became clear that John Stanislaus and May were determined to marry, John Stanislaus's mother decided to return to Cork for good. The wedding took place in her absence in May 1880, the same month that Parnell became the official leader of the Irish Parliamentary Party.

The Joyces' first home in Dublin was Ontario Terrace, near the Grand Canal, the same address where the fictional Leopold Bloom and his wife, Molly, would live. Their first child, born seven months after their marriage, died when he was eight days old. The following year, when the United Liberal Club closed, John Stanislaus, using his political friends to assist him, found work as a rate collector in Dublin. This was a kind of sinecure that had an average salary of £400 a year, about four times the average industrial wage, and included a pension. Soon after he began this job, Joyce's mother died, leaving him six tenanted properties in Cork, which brought in £500 a year. Thus by the time James Joyce was born, in February 1882, his parents were very well off and could expect a life of some comfort.

Having moved a number of times in the first two years of their marriage, the Joyces finally settled on Brighton Square in Rathgar, close to May's brother William and his wife, Josephine, who would become an important figure in the lives of the Joyce children until her death in 1924. While John Stanislaus could tolerate Josephine, his relations with most of his wife's family, including her brothers, did not improve. Stanislaus recounted that his father 'pursued' his father-in-law '(and when the old man died his memory) as well as [his wife's] family with an unrelenting hatred and unremitting virulent abuse that amounted to an obsession'.

Joyce's job meant that he had to get to know the city. His rate collecting included not only streets close to where he lived but the more sparsely populated areas around the Phoenix Park and along the coast to the south of the city. The job, which began at ten o'clock in the morning and finished at four in the afternoon, involved a great deal of travelling with no supervision over how long he stayed talking in a certain house or how he distracted himself throughout the day. It was the perfect job for someone who was social and garrulous. Since headquarters were in Fleet Street in the city centre, this meant that when work ended there were many public houses to choose between.

Besides some miscarriages, May Joyce had ten children. Between her marriage and her death in 1903, the family changed house as many times. The grandest place they lived was on Castlewood Avenue in Rathmines, a three-storey, double-fronted building where they moved in 1884, having been joined by an uncle of John Stanislaus from Cork and a woman called Mrs Conway, a devout Catholic, also from Cork, whom James Joyce would immortalize as Dante or Mrs Riordan in *A Portrait of the Artist as a Young Man*. In this house, John Stanislaus would entertain the rising class of Parnellites and his musical friends. He and his wife, as a fashionable couple, would attend operas and recitals in the city.

Despite his job and his rents, John Stanislaus Joyce, even in the early years of his marriage, had difficulty living within his means, and was forced to remortgage some of his property in Cork and borrow money to supplement his income. In 1887, having taken out a loan using a Cork property as collateral, Joyce moved his family to Bray, close to where the Wildes had owned houses.

At work, Joyce was also beginning to have problems. The authorities were sceptical when he claimed to have been attacked in the Phoenix Park and robbed of the cash that he had collected. He was transferred to the city centre, where it was easier to keep an eye on him and where he was often accompanied by an inspector. While he still enjoyed the freedom the job offered, he did not take any pleasure in the paperwork, which he often farmed out. Stanislaus reported that 'he would have a couple of unemployed old clerks scribbling in his house from morning to midnight' when deadlines approached. Subsequently, he was transferred to the city's docklands, including its busy red-light district.

When James Joyce was six, his parents sent him as a boarder to Clongowes Wood College, a posh school run by the Jesuits. Although his father had many friends and he and his wife were still involved in concerts and social outings, John Stanislaus's temper was not improved by his drinking. In *My Brother's Keeper*, his son recounted that in these years:

> at home he was a man of absolutely unreliable temper. How often do I remember him sitting at table in the evening, not exactly drunk – he carried his liquor too well then – but sufficiently so to have no appetite and to be in vile humour . . . In later years my mother told me that she was often terrified to be alone with him, although he was not normally a violent man . . . He would sit there grinding his teeth and looking at my mother and muttering

phrases like 'Better finish it now.' At one time she thought of getting a separation from him, but her confessor was so furious when she suggested it that she never mentioned it again.

John Stanislaus Joyce would remain throughout his life a staunch defender of Parnell, whose political career was coming to an end just as the Dublin Corporation Act was passed, which would allow the Corporation to collect the rates itself, thus putting Joyce's income as a rate collector in jeopardy. In the 1892 elections, after the death of Parnell, Joyce offered to work for the Parnellite candidate in Cork, telling his workplace that he was ill so that he could travel south. When he was spotted in Cork, he was reported to the Collector-General, which did not help his case in a position that was increasingly precarious.

Even though he still had his job, and despite the income from the properties, his finances became even more difficult, with moneylenders in pursuit and with rent overdue on the house in Blackrock where the family had moved from Bray. There were court judgments against him. Bailiffs seized his furniture, leaving him only the portraits of his parents and grandparents that his son James would eventually have transported to Trieste and proudly display.

Late in 1892 or early in 1893, Joyce was forced to move his family to the area around Mountjoy Square and the North Circular Road on the north side of Dublin. On 1 January 1893 almost all of his colleagues lost their jobs as rate collectors, but were offered a generous severance package: three-quarters of their annual salary as an annual pension, irrespective of how long they had served. Because of his poor record, however, this did not apply to John Stanislaus Joyce, who was at first offered nothing and then half of what his colleagues were getting. This amounted to only one-third of his former wage.

Thus at the age of forty-four, Joyce was living in a sort of aftermath. Having basked in the glory that came from being a supporter of Parnell, he was now left to linger in the dullness and rancour that came once the Irish Parliamentary Party had split. And, once more, he had to find odd jobs as an accountant or financial clerk or take any other work that came his way. At this stage, he had nine children to support. By the end of 1893, having remortgaged much of it and borrowed heavily on the strength of it, he was forced to sell all the property that he had inherited in Cork.

His sons James and Stanislaus were sent first to O'Connell School, run by the Christian Brothers, close to where they lived in Dublin. But soon Father Conmee, a Jesuit priest who had known James at Clongowes and who would be rewarded by a mention in *Ulysses*, arranged for them to attend the posher Belvedere College, a Jesuit day school, also close to where they lived.

\*

John Stanislaus Joyce was perhaps unlucky that he had lost his job, and unlucky too that he did not know how to manage his finances, and unlucky also that he had so many children to feed, but his worst piece of luck may have been the brooding presence in his household throughout his fall from grace of his second living son, Stanislaus, who charted what happened to the family with bitterness and in some detail in two books, both published after his death: *My Brother's Keeper* in 1958 and *The Complete Dublin Diary of Stanislaus Joyce*, published in 1971.

In the first of these, Stanislaus recalled the household once his father had lost his job and sold his properties:

> My father was still in his early forties, a man who had received a university education and had never known a day's illness. But though he had a large family of young children, he was quite

unburdened by any sense of responsibility towards them. His pension, which could have taken in part the place of the property he had lost and been a substantial addition to an earned income, became his and our only means of subsistence.

In his writings, Stanislaus wrote that the nine addresses where they lived over a period of at most eleven years, 'besides representing a descending step on the ladder of our fortunes,' were each of them associated in his memory 'with some particular phase of our gypsy-like family life'.

He described the method in his father's fecklessness:

Whenever a landlord could not put up with him any longer and wanted to get rid of him, [he went] to the landlord [to] say that it would be impossible for him with his rent in arrears to find a new house, and that it was indispensable that he should be able to show the receipts for the last few months' rent of the house he was living in. Then the landlord, to get a bad tenant off his hands, would give him receipts for the unpaid rent of a few months, and with these my father would be able to inveigle some other landlord into letting him a house. In these auspicious circumstances we moved into a smaller house in a poorer neighbourhood.

Stanislaus noted all the drunkenness and the outrages, including the scene where John Stanislaus Joyce 'made a vague attempt to strangle' his wife:

In a drunken fit he ran at her and seized her by the throat, roaring, 'Now, by God, is the time to finish it.' The children who were in the room ran screaming in between them, but my brother, with more presence of mind, sprang promptly on his back and overbalanced him so that they tumbled on the floor. My mother snatched

up the two youngest children and escaped with my elder sister to
our neighbour's house.

As James Joyce made his way through Belvedere College and
then to University College Dublin and later escaped to Paris,
Stanislaus kept a firm watch on his father. On 26 September 1903,
for example, he wrote of him in his diary:

> He is domineering and quarrelsome and has in an unusual degree
> that low, voluble abusiveness characteristic of the Cork people
> when drunk . . . He is lying and hypocritical. He regards himself
> as the victim of circumstances and pays himself with words. His
> will is dissipated and his intellect besotted, and he has become a
> crazy drunkard. He is spiteful like all drunkards who are thwarted,
> and invents the most cowardly insults that a scandalous mind and
> a naturally derisive tongue can suggest.

He noted also that 'When Pappie is sober and fairly comfortable
he is easy and pleasant spoken though inclined to sigh and complain
and do nothing. His conversation is reminiscent and humorous, ridi-
culing without malice, and accepting peace as an item of comfort.'

In April 1904, he noted: 'When there is money in this house it
is impossible to do anything because of Pappie's drunkenness
and quarrelling. When there is no money it is impossible to do
anything because of the hunger and cold and want of light.' In
another entry in the same month, he wrote: 'Pappie is a balking
little rat. His idea when he has money is that he has power over
those whom he should support, and his character is to bully
them, make them run after him, and in the end cheat them of
their wish. In his face this is featured in his O'Connell snout.'
(John Stanislaus's mother was an O'Connell.)

In July 1904, he wrote about the tension between his father and
James:

*Pappie has been drunk for the last three days. He has been*
*shouting about getting Jim's arse kicked. Always the one word.*
*'O yes! Kick him, by God! Break his arse with a kick, break his*
*bloody arse with three kicks. O yes! Just three kicks!' And so on*
*through torturous obscenity. I am sick of it, sick of it.*

On 6 August, he noted that 'there is no dinner in the house'.
His diary ends in January 1905. In its place, his younger brother
Charlie kept a diary beginning in May that year, a diary that made
its way to the library of Cornell University, and is quoted by John
Wyse Jackson and Peter Costello in their biography of John Stanislaus Joyce. On 26, 27 and 28 May, Charlie Joyce noted that his
father was drunk, and again on 31 May, 1, 2, 13, 14 and 15 June. And
on 24 June: 'Pappie home to dinner very drunk: shouting, swear-
ing etc. Pappie has thrown his dinner about the floor: Baby [the
youngest of the family] white as a sheet: Pappie gone out again:
home again: sleeping off some of the drunk.' Another entry
notes that one sister pawned her dress as there was no dinner.

By this time, Georgie Joyce, three years younger than Stanislaus and five years younger than James, had died a slow and
painful death at the age of fourteen, and May Joyce had died aged
forty-four. Perhaps of all the passages about their father by the
Joyce sons, the section in *My Brother's Keeper* about their mother's
deathbed, to which James had been summoned from Paris, is the
most harrowing:

My father was on his good behaviour for the first few weeks but
as the illness dragged on he became unreliable and had to be
watched. One evening towards the end, my father came home
'screwed', as Aunt Josephine called it, after having drowned his
sorrows copiously with various friends, and went into my
mother's room. Besides my aunt, my brother [James] and I were

both there. My father asked some perfunctory question, but it was evident that he was in vile humour and itching to say something. He walked about the room muttering and then, coming to the foot of the bed, he blurted out: 'I'm finished. I can't do any more. If you can't get well, die. Die and be damned to you!' Forgetting everything, I shouted 'You swine!' and made a swift movement towards him. Then to my horror I saw that my mother was struggling to get out of the bed. I hurried to her at once, while Jim led my father out of the room. 'You mustn't do that,' my mother panted. 'You must promise me never to do that, you know that when he is that way he doesn't know what he is saying.'

Stanislaus Joyce left for Trieste to join his brother, who had gone to live there. Charlie went to Boston for a while and then returned to Dublin with his wife and raised a large family in the city.

The girls in the Joyce family kept no diaries, as far as we know, and they wrote no memoirs, but as soon as they could, two of them went to Trieste, one returning soon afterwards. One joined a convent and spent the rest of her life in New Zealand. The others found work in Dublin, and, as soon as possible, they left home. Some of them had very little to do with their father again and felt a deep anger against him. He had blighted their lives.

Once his youngest daughter died at the age of eighteen in 1911, according to his biographers, John Stanislaus Joyce 'could no longer endure living with his daughters and their reproaches, spoken and unspoken. His relations with them had become actively hostile in all directions.'

From 1920 until his death in 1931, John Stanislaus Joyce lived alone in a boarding house where he maintained, it seemed, cordial relations with the landlady. For the last nineteen years of his life he did not see his son James, since he did not return to Ireland, nor indeed did Stanislaus see any reason to come back from

Trieste to visit his father in old age. All that was left in his room when the old man died, the landlady's husband reported, was 'an old suit of clothes, a coat, hat, boots and stick' and a copy of his son's play *Exiles*.

*

It would be easy then to consign John Stanislaus Joyce to the position of one of the worst Irish husbands and worst Irish fathers in recorded history. But because James Joyce wished to, or sought to, deal with his father's legacy and his father's life in his work, and because he had moved away from him and lived with his memories, another picture emerges. Instead of actively and openly killing his father, James Joyce sought not only to memorialize his father but also to retrace his steps, enter his spirit, use what he needed from his father's life to nourish his own art.

In his introduction to *My Brother's Keeper*, T. S. Eliot remarks that the book 'has the quality of candour which reminds me of Gosse's *Father and Son*'. Stanislaus's memoir has a raw sense of grievance, at times against both James and his father. It should have been possible, then, for a writer as talented and determined as his brother to have made an entire career out of his anger at his father, to have forged in the smithy of his soul a portrait of his country in the guise of his drunken and wayward father, which the world would have assented to and recognized, while feeling his pain.

There is something radiant and oddly magnificent, however, in Joyce's refusing this temptation, in deciding that he had other onions to fry.

But this refusal can be seen also as an aspect of his single-mindedness. Added to this, he might not have suffered as much as his other siblings. In describing his father's drunken antics in *My Brother's Keeper*, Stanislaus noted:

My brother was less affected by these scenes than I was, though they certainly influenced his attitude towards marriage and family life . . . That attachment to his father, which was to be one of the dominant motives in his character, remained unchanged. When he went up to Clongowes, the home he left was moderately prosperous and happy. He came back to it when a holiday atmosphere prevailed at Christmas and, as well as I remember, at Easter, and during the long summer vacation . . . As he remained in college until he was almost ten, he knew only the more gracious aspect of our family life, the more amiable side of my father's character.

Later, he noted, James Joyce, while at school in Dublin, would spend the evenings reading in his room, paying no attention to his father or anybody else. He also remarked that 'justice towards the characters of his own creation, or imaginative re-creation, became an artistic principle' with his brother.

There is an interesting moment in Stanislaus's diary where he, too, attempts to do justice to the father that he generally loathes. He notes that his father's relationship with him and his brother is something he misses in how fathers relate to their sons in other households. 'I think it is this,' he wrote, 'that he wishes and confidently expects that his sons will be different from the sons of other people, even – and this shows a yet higher mind – more distinguished than he, in his own judgment.'

In the margins, he added:

Moreover, he has always treated us with a kind of equality with an item or two of authority, and did not think it fit to do away with all ordinary politeness in dealing with us. He has tacitly respected our privacy and has not treated us with that contemptuous inconsiderateness, as towards animals, by which fathers try silently to insist on their absolute superiority. He has not been able to be a senseless bully, and we have no reason not to respect him for what he is – our father.

It is important to note that this is a diary entry for July 1904 rather than something conjured up in retrospect to explain his brother's genius.

After his father's death, James Joyce wrote of him to T. S. Eliot:

*He had an intense love for me and it adds anew to my grief and remorse that I did not go to Dublin to see him for so many years. I kept him constantly under the illusion that I would come and was always in correspondence with him but an instinct I believed in held me back from going, much as I longed to.*

To his benefactor Harriet Weaver, Joyce wrote:

*I was very fond of him always, being a sinner myself, and even liked his faults. Hundreds of pages and scores of characters in my books came from him . . . I got from him his portraits, a waistcoat, a good tenor voice, and an extravagant licentious disposition (out of which, however, the greater part of any talent I may have springs) but, apart from these, something else I cannot define.*

He told his friend Louis Gillet in Paris: 'The humour of *Ulysses* is his; its people are his friends. The book is his spittin' image.'

Since we have so much evidence about John Stanislaus Joyce as a father, it is fascinating to watch as his son set about making art from the threadbare and often miserable business of what he knew, what he had experienced, and who his father was. In his work, James Joyce allowed a complex imagination to shine its pale, unsettled light on what had already passed into shade so that he could coax it back into substance, courtesy of style.

As he began the process, however, it is important to note that he was tentative. He dealt with his father's legacy in ways that wavered and moved against each other.

In his original plan for *Dubliners*, the last story was to be 'Grace', written in October 1905. The story begins with a real event that happened to Joyce's father when he fell down the stairs of John Nolan's public house in Harry Street off Grafton Street on his way to the lavatory. He was rescued by a friend of his, Tom Devin, who was an official in Dublin Corporation. As he imagined the story, Joyce changed the background of Mr Kernan, the man who falls, from that of his father to a neighbour of the Joyces' called Dick Thornton, a tea taster and an opera lover. The story of the religious retreat that occurs in 'Grace' was provided to Joyce by Stanislaus, who had followed his father and some of his friends to such a retreat in Gardiner Street Church.

In his diary for 29 September 1904, Stanislaus wrote:

> The last time Pappie went to Confession and Communion was highly amusing. I bawled laughing at the time. It was about two years ago. Mr Kane and Mr Boyd and Mr Chance [Kane becoming Martin Cunningham in *Dubliners* and *Ulysses*; Boyd also mentioned by name in *Ulysses*, and Chance in *Finnegans Wake*] were to attend a retreat in Gardiner Street, and Pappie, who would never do anything so vulgar himself, was persuaded by Mr Kane to attend it too. He did so and came home very drunk for two nights after each sermon.

When his father went to Confession, he came home and announced that the priest had told him that he 'wasn't such a bad fellow after all'.

The tone of the story 'Grace' is unsparing, unmerciful. The drinker's clothes 'were smeared with the filth and ooze of the floor on which he had lain, face downwards. His eyes were closed and he breathed with a grunting noise.'

The use of a style that is forensic continues as, having taken the drunk man home, 'Two nights after, his friends came to see him' as he was in bed and they began to discuss religion. When they mention the name of a priest who will lead the retreat, Father Purdon, the Dublin reader will get the joke, as Purdon Street was one of the best-known streets in Dublin's red-light district – it will be named in the Nighttown section of *Ulysses* – but the men themselves are not aware of how funny this is. Nor are they alert to their own foolishness as they muse on the various popes and their mottos from Lux upon Lux to Crux upon Crux. And at the retreat itself as they peer at a speck of red light suspended before the high altar and are preached to by Father Purdon, they are comic figures, worthy of our mockery. The jokes in the story happen because of their ignorance, their insularity, the clichés they use. They have no wit, no energy.

Had *Dubliners* ended there, Joyce would have taken a suitable revenge on his father and mocked his father's friends, and allowed the reader in on the joke. The figures in 'Grace', even the priest in his sermon, speak in tired, dead voices. 'The Dead' would have been a worthy title for a story in which the idea of grace is presented ironically.

Two years later, when Joyce wrote 'The Dead', which eventually became the last story in *Dubliners*, it was as though he sought to resurrect those whom he had buried with mockery and distancing in 'Grace'. Instead of studying the main character as though for his own amusement, he entered his spirit, allowed him to have a complex sensibility and a rich response to experience.

The story was also based on an event in his father's life, but this time instead of recounting it, Joyce began to dream it, reimagine

it, and offer it a sort of grace that the previous story had significantly lacked.

\*

This idea of fully imagining events that had occurred in the lives
of the previous generation is analysed in the opening of an essay
on Seán Ó Faoláin by Conor Cruise O'Brien in his book *Maria
Cross*. In Joyce's last years in Dublin, both he and Stanislaus spent
time in the house of the Sheehy family, whose father was an MP
for the Irish Parliamentary Party, and they got to know some of
the daughters in that house, one of whom, Kathleen, was the
mother of Conor Cruise O'Brien. The figure of Miss Ivors in
'The Dead' was partly based on her.

In much of Conor Cruise O'Brien's own writing about Ireland,
there is a sense of a twilight time after the fall of Parnell and
before the 1916 Rebellion, when his mother's family, the Sheehys,
held power in Dublin, a time that Cruise O'Brien seemed to
inhabit with considerable ease and a sort of longing, a time that
is also when Joyce imagined his Dublin.

Cruise O'Brien wrote:

> There is for all of us a twilight zone of time, stretching back for a
> generation or two before we were born, which never quite belongs to
> the rest of history. Our elders have talked their memories into our
> memories until we come to possess some sense of a continuity
> exceeding and traversing our own individual being . . . Children of
> small and vocal communities are likely to possess it to a high degree
> and, if they are imaginative, have the power of incorporating into
> their own lives a significant span of time before their individual births.

This twilight zone of time entered the spirit of 'The Dead' in
fascinating ways, as Joyce set his story not only in an imagined

past but also in an imagined future. In the time between writing 'Grace' and writing 'The Dead', scrupulous meanness in Joyce gave way to a hesitant, hushed generosity. In abandoning his siblings' version of his father, he managed to release a great deal of psychic energy, which allowed him then to experiment with form and style, to move subsequently from the hesitant and the hushed into a fictional system that was brave and comic and untempered by caution.

He had not attended those parties in Usher's Island, the parties described in 'The Dead'. In *My Brother's Keeper*, Stanislaus wrote: 'My father and mother had many friends in Bray and in town, and at about Christmas time and New Year they often went up to dances in Dublin and stayed overnight at a hotel, as the Conroys do in "The Dead".' He also noted that his father had a 'glib tongue' as a public speaker. 'As for his "gift of the gab", excepting the literary allusions which Gabriel Conroy considers above the head of his listeners, the speech in "The Dead" is a fair sample, somewhat polished and emended, of his after-dinner oratory.'

In his biography of Joyce, Richard Ellmann wrote:

The other festival occasions of [James Joyce's] childhood were associated with his hospitable great-aunts, Mrs Callanan and Mrs Lyons, and Mrs Callanan's daughter Mary Ellen at their house at 15 Usher's Island, which was also known as the 'Misses Flynn school'. There every year the Joyces who were old enough would go, and John Joyce carved the goose and made the speech.

The quarrel between Gabriel and his mother about his marriage in 'The Dead' has elements of the quarrel between John Stanislaus and his mother when he married May Murray.

However, the figure of Gabriel has elements in common with James Joyce himself as well as his father. Gabriel writes book reviews for the *Daily Express*, as Joyce did. His wife is from the west of Ireland, as Nora Barnacle was. Gabriel is a teacher, as James Joyce was. He has cosmopolitan tendencies rather than nationalist sympathies, as Joyce did.

Ellmann also suggested, using Stanislaus Joyce as a source, that there could be another model for Gabriel, a friend of Joyce called Constantine Curran, and he offers some possible evidence for this, including Curran's uneasy personality and the fact that Gabriel's brother in the story is called Constantine.

But it is more likely that Joyce found details wherever he needed them. He was not working from precise models. He began by imagining that house on Usher's Island, and the twilight time for him when his parents, as a glamorous young couple that he saw depart from the house in Bray, went there, a couple united in their love of song, gifted with good singing voices. He gave his father a rich dignity in the story. It is Freddy Malins who was drunk, not Gabriel. He imagined his parents' night in all its glowing detail; he saw who else was there; he saw how the evening moved and how it ended.

He saw this so clearly that he entered its spirit until he began to walk himself in those rooms in the footsteps of his father. He saw his own partner, Nora Barnacle, there in the place of his mother, or in the guise of his mother. He saw himself in the guise of his father. He merged his own spirit with that of his father, as he would do later with the river at the end of *Finnegans Wake*: 'it's sad and weary I go back to you, my cold father, my cold mad father, my cold mad feary father', as he invokes his father in the very last lines of *A Portrait of the Artist as a Young Man*: 'Old father, old artificer, stand me now and ever in good stead.'

He moved both himself and his father out of time in 'The Dead'. To do this, he needed to make a third character, who is the writer of the story, who, as Joyce with the white page in front of him attempts this grand act of emotional recuperation, wavers in his style, begins in a tone of pure colloquialism, like someone casually telling a story, and ends in a tone of high artifice that is close to the language of pre-Raphaelite poetry or Victorian prayer. It begins with the isolated figure of Lily, the caretaker's daughter, who quickly disappears, and ends with 'all the living and the dead'.

In between, the point of view and the texture of noticed things in the story shift and change. And Gabriel's very uneasiness, his watchfulness, his in-betweenness, operate as a writer does who is attempting to do something new. Nothing is lost on him, least of all his own sense of inadequacy, his own sense of need. Just as Gabriel is unsure that his speech is suitable for the occasion, the story itself is unsure, unwilling to settle into a single tone.

Gabriel is tentative, as much a ghost as Michael Furey is. He is caught between two identities, his Irish one and his efforts to escape insularity, as Joyce is caught now between two visions of his father, the one he knows and remembers, and the other that he wishes to bring into being in order to rescue his imagination from a sense of narrow grievance that is capable only of debasing and maiming that same imagination.

The opening sentence of the second-last paragraph of 'The Dead' reads: 'Generous tears filled Gabriel's eyes.' In the mixing of his own sensuality with his imagination of his father's sensuality, in allowing his own ghost to mingle with that of John Stanislaus Joyce, he banished his scrupulous meanness and performed an act of generosity. He rescued himself for the work that he would now make.

But it was still tentative. There is a wonderfully tender passage in Joyce's *Stephen Hero*, the early version of *A Portrait of the Artist as a Young Man*, when Stephen the son, who is attending university, asks his mother if she would like him to read out to her an essay he has written on Ibsen. When she assents: 'Stephen read out the essay to her slowly and emphatically and when he had finished reading she said it was very beautifully written but that as there were some things in it which she couldn't follow, would he mind reading it to her again and explaining some of it.'

When he has finished, she expresses an interest in reading Ibsen's best play. 'But do you really want to read Ibsen?' Stephen said. His mother replies: 'I do, really.' A few moments later, she says: 'Before I married your father I used to read a great deal. I used to take an interest in all kinds of new plays.'

In *Stephen Hero*, Mrs Daedalus begins to read Ibsen:

> A day or two afterwards Stephen gave his mother a few of the plays to read. She read them with great interest and found Nora Helmer a charming character. Dr Stockmann she admired but her admiration was naturally checked by her son's light-heartedly blasphemous description of that stout burgher as 'Jesus in a frock-coat'. But the play which she preferred to all others was *The Wild Duck*. Of it she spoke readily and on her own initiative: it had moved her deeply.

When Stephen tries to patronize her, by hoping she is not going to compare Hedvig Ekdal to Little Nell in *The Old Curiosity Shop*, she responds: 'Of course I like Dickens too but I can see a great difference between Little Nell and that poor little creature . . .' She goes on to say that Ibsen's plays 'have impressed me very much' and that she thinks they were 'magnificent plays indeed'. When her son asks if she thinks them immoral, she replies: 'I think that Ibsen . . . has an extraordinary knowledge of human nature . . . And I think that human nature is a very extraordinary thing sometimes.'

In *Stephen Hero*, Stephen is also confronted directly by his mother about his loss of faith. She is fervent and fully present in the scene, a person with firm beliefs and with a conscience as insistent as that of her son. What we get from her in *Stephen Hero* is a hurt stubbornness, which matches her son's.

While Stephen's mother in *Stephen Hero* is thus presented as intelligent, open-minded and sensitive, as well as a devout and serious Catholic who pays attention to her priest, Stephen's father is depicted as hard-hearted and callous as he responds coldly to the return home of his daughter, Isabel, who will die in the novel:

> Stephen's father did not like the prospect of another inhabitant in his house, particularly a daughter for whom he had little affection. He was annoyed that his daughter would not avail herself of the opportunity afforded her in the convent, but his sense of public duty was real if spasmodic and he would by no means permit his wife to bring the girl home without his aid . . . Stephen's father was quite capable of talking himself into believing what he knew to be untrue. He knew that his own ruin had been his own handiwork but he had talked himself into believing that it was the handiwork of others. He had his son's distaste for responsibility without his son's courage.

He was in danger, we are told, 'of becoming a monomaniac. The hearth at night was the sacred witness of these revenges, pondered, muttered, growled and execrated.'

Later, the book describes Mr Daedalus's attitude towards paying rent:

> Mr Daedalus had not an acute sense of the rights of private property: he paid rent very rarely. To demand money for eatables seemed to him just but to expect people to pay for shelter the exorbitant sums which are demanded annually by house-owners in Dublin seemed to him unjust. He had now been a year in his house in Clontarf and for that year he had paid a quarter's rent.

Later in the book also, Stephen is abused by his father for not studying hard enough ('the sooner you clear out the better') and for turning down an offer of paid work that the Jesuits had made him. His father calls him an 'unnatural bloody ruffian' and expresses his shame at seeing him drinking a pint of stout with the hearse drivers after his sister's funeral. ('By Christ I was ashamed of you that morning.')

What is fascinating here is how the tones in which the parents are described change from *Stephen Hero* to *A Portrait of the Artist as a Young Man*. In the later book, the figure of the mother will have no interest other than domestic peace, household activities and religion. She is no longer the sensitive woman who could respond to reading Ibsen or who can argue with her son about his loss of faith. Her agency has been relinquished, she has been consigned to cliché, to the background of the book, so that other dynamics, most notably those connected with her son's startling growth of conscience and ambition, can be fully exploited.

These energies will allow the figure of the mother to be resurrected with haunting urgency in the pages of *Ulysses*. But it is as though a full confrontation with her has been wilfully postponed.

Just as the scenes with the mother are rendered more ordinary in *A Portrait*, so, too, the father's impecuniousness is not analysed glibly or easily there. The son's relationship with his father is presented in real time as something oddly mysterious and painful, evoking a tone that is melancholy, puzzled, almost poetic. There is none of the certainty of a sentence like: 'Mr Daedalus had not an acute sense of the rights of private property: he paid rent very rarely,' a sentence that is very pleased with itself and sure of what it wishes to achieve.

In *A Portrait*, on the other hand, in the scene where they have moved house, the tone is that from a book about the making of a poet rather than the unmasking of a father:

Stephen sat on a footstool beside his father listening to a long and incoherent monologue. He understood little or nothing of it at first but he became slowly aware that his father had enemies and that some fight was going to take place. He felt too that he was being enlisted for the fight, that some duty was being laid upon his shoulders. The sudden flight from the comfort and revery of Blackrock, the passage through the gloomy foggy city, the thought of the bare cheerless house in which they were now to live made his heart heavy . . .

When his father's speech is quoted, it comes like this: 'There's a crack of the whip left in me yet, Stephen, old chap, said Mr Dedalus, poking at the dull fire with fierce energy. We're not dead yet, sonny. No, by the Lord Jesus (God forgive me) nor half dead.'

This scene, and a later scene in the book when the family moves house once more, are rendered in slow time. In the earlier book, we get sentences like: 'Stephen's father was quite capable of talking himself into believing what he knew to be untrue.' Compared to this piece of firm judgment, the description of the father in the later book withholds easy conclusions. Character is created not by statements but by suggestions, not by verdicts but by stray images that form a dense, open-ended pattern.

Joyce rescues his father from the sort of certainty that Stanislaus uses in his diary and his memoir and from the tone that he himself adopts in *Stephen Hero* by moving his father from the private realm, where he clearly is a bully and a monster, into the public sphere. He allows him to be the man he is with his friends rather than with his family. He sees what can be done by dramatizing the friction between Simon Dedalus and a world he enjoys somewhat but does not fully control.

Towards the end of *A Portrait*, Stephen is asked by his friend Cranly the precise question about his father that Gretta is asked by Gabriel in 'The Dead' about Michael Furey. 'What was he?' In 'The Dead', Gretta's answer will come with a soft innocence: 'He was in the gasworks.' In *A Portrait*, Stephen's reply is filled with comic energy, as though his father is a character in a novel, and his attributes are something almost to be proud of, and all the better for being true: 'A medical student, an oarsman, a tenor, an amateur actor, a shouting politician, a small landlord, a small investor, a drinker, a good fellow, a storyteller, somebody's secretary, something in a distillery, a taxgatherer, a bankrupt and at present a praiser of his own past.'

But even though the figure of the father in *A Portrait* comes to us with greater sympathy and tolerance and shade than in *Stephen Hero*, he is not to be presented as a model citizen or a father to be proud of. The two other scenes in which his conflicted self and ways of confronting the world are dramatized have different kinds of force.

The first is the Christmas Day scene that happens early in the book in which both Mrs Riordan on one side of the argument about Parnell and the Fenian Mr Casey on the other are more extreme and intemperate than Simon Dedalus, although Simon Dedalus makes his own position very clear, and, courtesy of sharp wit and persistence, brings the reader with him so that it seems to the reader, as to his son, that he has won the day and routed Mrs Riordan and all other enemies of freedom.

The texture of his dialogue here is crisp and rational. When Simon says of the church: 'They have only themselves to blame . . . If they took a fool's advice they would confine their attention to religion,' it is added that he said this 'suavely'. This is not a word that Stanislaus Joyce would use to modify his description of his father's sayings. Later in the argument, the modifying word for another of Stephen's father's interjections is 'coolly'.

Simon manages to serve the dinner in the middle of all the acrimony, winking at his son so as to make him his ally. It is only after much care and holding back and provocation that he finally 'threw his knife and fork noisily on his plate'. It is at this point only that the modifier 'coarsely' is used about his speech. After that, however, he can return to being good-humoured quite easily, as indeed he can continue the argument without invective or abuse. There is no question of his being the worse for drink. He maintains a sort of dignity throughout the scene.

In the end, it is Mr Casey who shouts 'No God for Ireland!', not Mr Dedalus. In fact, Mr Dedalus, as a figure of reason, tries to restrain him from further intemperate speech and he and Uncle Charles pull him back into the chair again, 'talking to him from both sides reasonably'. And rather than hearing his father shout further, Stephen, 'raising his terror-stricken face, saw that his father's eyes were full of tears'. He is crying for the one thing that his son also will feel reverence for throughout his life – the memory of Charles Stewart Parnell.

The other scene with his father in *A Portrait* moves completely out of the domestic sphere as Stephen accompanies a more wayward figure of a father to Cork, so that his father can revisit old places, rekindle memories, drink a great deal and also sell his properties by auction.

From the beginning of the journey, Stephen is uncomfortable with his father. 'He listened without sympathy to his father's evocation of Cork and of scenes of his youth, a tale broken by sighs or draughts from his pocketflask whenever the image of some dead friend appeared in it or whenever the evoker remembered suddenly the purpose of his actual visit. Stephen heard but could feel no pity.'

Because his father's sojourn in Cork is presented as shameful and maudlin, he emerges as pathetic rather than strong, sad rather than bullying, tedious rather than frightening. As he moves with him, Stephen does not come to loathe his father, nor even despise him. That would be too easy and fixed; it would not serve his purpose. Instead, he listens and watches and lets his mind wander. Stray words come to him powerfully, but also confusingly, and fragments of poetry. And also guilt about how he himself feels or who he has become fills his mind, as the conversation around him in all its futility goes on.

There is too much else happening in his delicate consciousness, and the range of his anxieties is too great, for him to be able to make the easy judgments about his father that were made in *Stephen Hero*. The gaze is always inwards. But nonetheless his father is not honoured or exalted in this scene as he drinks with his friend. His very weakness allows Stephen to feel that his own 'mind seemed older than theirs: it shone coldly on their strifes and happiness and regrets like a moon upon a younger earth'. It is not merely that he is growing up in these scenes, but rather he is becoming wiser than his father ever was, he is more filled with watchfulness and nerves and depth of feeling than his father ever will be.

★

Having learned to observe his father in a story such as 'Grace' and in *Stephen Hero*, and having merged his spirit with that of his father in 'The Dead', in *A Portrait of the Artist as a Young Man*, Joyce now sought to outsoar his father, to see him as if through sweetened air from high above. He has become Icarus, the son of Daedalus, but an Icarus who will fly to avoid what will seek to ensnare him, who will declare: 'When the soul of a man is born in this country there are nets flung at it to hold it back from flight. You talk to me of nationality, language, religion. I shall try to fly by those nets.'

As he flies, however, he will be followed by his father, the figure evoked in the very last sentence of his portrait of himself as a young man.

Simon Dedalus appears or is mentioned in seven of the eighteen episodes of *Ulysses*. In some of the earlier versions we have of him, whether as John Stanislaus Joyce in *My Brother's Keeper* or in the biography of him by Wyse Jackson and Costello, once he is at home, he is fully ostracized, but when we meet him first in the Hades episode of *Ulysses* he is fully socialized. He is in a carriage with other men on his way to Paddy Dignam's funeral.

As they travel to the funeral, they catch sight of Stephen Dedalus, 'your son and heir', as Leopold Bloom points out. As Simon Dedalus rants for a while about the company his son is keeping and what he intends to do about it, this is a moment when it is open to Joyce to establish that Simon is seen as a crank by his companions. Thus Bloom muses: 'Noisy selfwilled man.'

But then, making clear that he does not see Simon in the same way as Stanislaus Joyce sees his father, Bloom follows: 'Full of his son. He is right.' Twice, as he speaks, Simon Dedalus is given a good sharp line of dialogue, thus establishing him as a man who is witty or has a way with words. The first is when he says of Buck Mulligan: 'I'll tickle his catastrophe.' The second is when he announces that the weather is 'as uncertain as a child's bottom'.

In order to anchor the figure of Simon Dedalus in the life of his own father, Joyce then quickly allows a moment in which Reuben J. Dodd, someone from his father's actual life, a man to whom John Stanislaus owed money and whom he disliked intensely, appears on the street. Simon Dedalus says: 'The devil break the hasp of your back!'

The modifier here for the verb 'said' is 'mildly', and it is significant. Simon Dedalus does not shout at the man or bark the abuse; he does not embarrass his companions in the carriage by roaring at the man. However, he makes his views known to them as they discuss Dodd, saying that 'I wish to Christ' that Dodd would drown and calling him 'that confirmed bloody hobbledehoy'.

Thus by the time he has arrived at Glasnevin Cemetery, Simon has already had two outbursts, however controlled, one against his son and the other against the man who lent him money. For the rest of the journey and in the graveyard itself, nonetheless, he is dignified and treated with respect by those whom he meets.

163

When the question arises if Dignam, who had died suddenly, was a heavy drinker, Simon Dedalus says: 'Many a good man's fault,' and it is noted that he said this with 'a sigh'. Soon, he thinks of his dead wife – May Joyce had died in 1903, a year before the time the novel is set:

> – Her grave is over there, Jack, Mr Dedalus said. I'll soon be stretched beside her. Let Him take me whenever He likes.
>
> Breaking down, he began to weep to himself quietly, stumbling a little in his walk. Mr Power took his arm.
>
> – She's better where she is, he said kindly.
>
> – I suppose so, Mr Dedalus said with a weak gasp. I suppose she is in heaven if there is a heaven.

The next time we see Simon Dedalus he is in the offices of the *Freeman's Journal*, and once more he is in company where he feels comfortable, comfortable enough to exclaim 'Agonising Christ, wouldn't it give you a heartburn on your arse?' when he is read a piece of overblown writing on the subject of Ireland. Soon he is quoting Byron. And not long after that he is 'giving vent to a hopeless groan' and crying 'shite and onions!' before putting on his hat and announcing: 'I must get a drink after that.'

Soon, however, the real world, or the world of Simon Dedalus's unfortunate family, makes itself felt, as two of his daughters talk in the kitchen of his house, one of them remarking: 'Crickey, is there nothing for us to eat?' as the other sister asks where their sibling Dilly is. 'Gone to meet father,' she is told. The other sister replies: 'Our father who art not in heaven.'

Later, close to an auctioneer's house, the afflicted Dilly meets her afflicted father and asks him for money. 'Where would I get money?' he asks. 'There is no-one in Dublin would lend me fourpence.' Dilly does not believe him. Eventually, he hands her a shilling and when she asks for more, he offers her a tirade of abuse: 'You're like the rest of them, are you? An insolent pack of little bitches since your poor mother died. But wait awhile. You'll all get a short shrift and a long day from me. Low blackguardism! I'm going to get rid of you. Wouldn't care if I was stretched out stiff. He's dead. The man upstairs is dead.'

Eventually, he gives her two more pennies and says that he will be home soon. Thus he has been placed in the position of a man whose children do not have enough money for food as he himself moves easily in the city. A man more at home with his companions and acquaintances than with his family.

When he appears next, in the company of a man called Cowley, it is significant that Cowley is in even worse financial straits than he is, and is being pursued by Dedalus's nemesis Reuben J. Dodd, to whom he owes money. When another man appears, Simon can make fun of him for his poor dress.

These encounters soften the previous one, or offer a context for it, establishing that to owe money and fear the bailiff and be poor are not attributes that belong to Dedalus alone, as they are treated almost lightly. The scene with Cowley further socializes, normalizes Simon Dedalus.

Up to this, however, he has been merely part of the day, another figure who wanders in the book, but in the next episode, Sirens, which takes place in the bar and restaurant of the Ormond Hotel on Ormond Quay, a building now sadly derelict, he moves towards the centre. The bar of this hotel was a place where Joyce, during his final visit to Dublin in 1912, had regularly met his father, who was working in some capacity for his friend the solicitor George Lidwell, who had offices nearby, and whose business address John Stanislaus was using as his address. Lidwell also advised James Joyce on the problems he was having with the putative publishers of *Dubliners*.

On 21 August 1912, Joyce wrote to Stanislaus in Trieste reporting on the jokes and stories he had heard while in the company of

Lidwell and his father in the bar of the Ormond Hotel. 'Pappie told them this story,' he wrote:

> *A bishop visited a P. P. [parish priest] and stayed too late to go home. The P. P. asked him to stay and said that there were only two beds in the house, his own and that of his housekeeper. The bishop said he would sleep in the P. P.'s bed for one night. They went to bed. In the morning the P. P. half awoke and hit the bishop a slap on the backside saying: – Get up Mary Ann, I'll be late for mass – And, by God, the very next day His Grace was made an archbishop.*

In *Ulysses*, at four o'clock in the afternoon, Simon Dedalus, in the Ormond Hotel, having flirted with the waitress, orders a half-glass of whiskey and some fresh water and lights up his pipe. Soon, his friend Lenehan puts his head around the door, and eventually greets him with: 'Greetings from the famous son of a famous father.' And when asked who this is, he replies: 'Stephen, the youthful bard.'

Mr Dedalus, famous father, laid by his dry filled pipe.

– I see, he said, I didn't recognize him for the moment. I hear he is keeping very select company. Have you seen him lately?

He had.

– I quaffed the nectarbowl with him this very day, said Lenehan. In Mooney's *en ville* and in Mooney's *sur mer*. He had received the rhino for the labour of his muse.

He smiled at bronze's teabathed lips, at listening lips and eyes.

– The *élite* of Erin hung upon his lips. The ponderous pundit. Hugh MacHugh, Dublin's most brilliant scribe and editor and that minstrel boy of the wild wet west who is known by the euphonious appellation of the O'Madden Burke.

After an interval Mr Dedalus raised his grog and

– That must have been highly diverting, said he. I see.

He see. He drank. With faraway mourning mountain eye. Set down his glass.

He looked towards the saloon door.

The 'rhino' referred to here is money. So it is clear that Stephen has money. And he is spending it with Hugh MacHugh, whom Simon Dedalus has seen earlier in the offices of the *Freeman's Journal*. O'Madden Burke is also a journalist. Hugh MacHugh would have been recognizable to readers as Hugh McNeill; O'Madden Burke is based on William O'Leary Curtis, a well-known journalist, whom James Joyce and his brother knew.

Since Simon Dedalus's tone is usually filled with wit and texture, his two responses here, 'That must have been highly diverting' and 'I see', witness him at his most subdued. He is neither the disliked father nor the easy companion; rather, he is the spurned father whose son does not seek his company, but who spends his time amusing more interesting people. Simon's 'faraway mourning mountain eye' is mourning the loss of Stephen, who has discarded him.

It would be easy then to have him ruminate on this loss for the rest of the chapter, order more drinks and feel sorry for himself before going home to annoy his daughters. But Joyce wishes to create in Simon a complex figure of moods, an unsettled rather than a solid presence in the book. As well as possessing a talent for not having money, Simon has, as Joyce's father did, a great tenor voice. In the rest of the chapter, as Bloom ruminates on many matters in the bar of the Ormond Hotel, and George Lidwell, whose real name is used, joins the company, Simon Dedalus and his companions move towards the piano, Simon manages to make a lewd joke about Molly Bloom, and then he sings 'M'appari' from Flotow's *Martha*: 'Through the hush of air a voice sang to them, low, not rain, not leaves in murmur, like no voice of strings or reeds or whatdoyoucallthem dulcimers, touching their still ears with words, still hearts of their each his remembered lives. Good, good to hear: sorrow from them each seemed to from both depart when first they heard.'

As Bloom listens, the novel tells us, 'the voice rose, sighing, changed: loud, full, shining, proud'. This is Simon Dedalus at his most exalted. Bloom notes the 'Glorious tone he has still. Cork air softer also their brogue.' Once more, Joyce, in this portrait of his father as an artist, has moved him to becoming Simon Hero among his friends.

But Joyce will never let anything happen for long. As Bloom watches Simon, he muses: 'Silly man! Could have made oceans of money.' And then in one pithy phrase, he returns the soaring singer to earth: 'Wore out his wife: now sings.'

When Simon finishes, he is greeted not only with applause but also with memories of other times when he sang, as Richie Goulding, Simon's brother-in-law,

> remembered one night long ago. Never forget that night. Si sang *'Twas rank and fame*: in Ned Lambert's 'twas. Good God he never heard in all his life a note like that he never did *then false one we had better part* so clear so God he never heard *since love lives not* a clinking voice ask Lambert he can tell you too.

Simon Dedalus, after his moment of apotheosis in the book, in the company of Ben Dollard, also remembers Italians singing in Cork: 'He heard them as a boy in Ringabella, Crosshaven, Ringabella, singing their barcaroles. Queenstown harbour full of Italian ships. Walking, you know, Ben, in the moonlight with those earthquake hats. Blending their voices. God, such music, Ben. Heard as a boy. Cross Ringabella haven mooncarole.'

Simon Dedalus praises Ben Dollard after he sings 'The Croppy

Boy'. Then the last time he will speak in *Ulysses*, as a mortal, will be when he muses 'The wife has a fine voice' when he hears that Bloom has been among the company. The rest of the novel will belong to Bloom and to Stephen.

The father will have been sent on his way as his son moves through the city in search of a surrogate for him.

Simon will, however, appear again in the Circe episode, in the phantasmagoria that takes place in the brothel. He will be wearing 'strong ponderous buzzard wings' and will ask Stephen to 'Think of your mother's people!' before, in a moment of extraordinary beauty, Stephen's mother, 'emaciated, rises stark through the floor in leper grey with a wreath of faded orange blossoms and a torn bridal veil, her face worn and noseless, green with grave mould. Her hair is scant and lank. She fixes her bluecircled hollow eyesockets on Stephen and opens her toothless mouth uttering a silent word.' Having said some words in Latin, wearing 'the subtle smile of death's madness', she will say: 'I was once the beautiful May Goulding. I am dead.' She will ask Stephen to repent, and suggest that he get his sister Dilly 'to make you that boiled rice every night after your brainwork'. When she says: 'Beware! God's hand!' a 'green crab with malignant red eyes sticks deep its grinning claws in Stephen's heart'.

'Strangled with rage', he will call out the word 'Shite!' as 'His features grow drawn and grey and old.'

In the next episode, Bloom remarks to Stephen that he has met his father earlier in the day, adding that he has gathered in the course of the conversation that he has moved house and asking where he is living. 'I believe he is in Dublin somewhere, Stephen answered unconcernedly. Why?'

Bloom goes on: 'A gifted man . . . in more respects than one and a born *raconteur* if ever there was one. He takes great pride, quite legitimately, out of you.' He suggests that Stephen might return to live with his father:

There was no response forthcoming to the suggestion, however, such as it was, Stephen's mind's eye being too busily engaged in repicturing his family hearth the last time he saw it, with his sister Dilly sitting by the ingle, her hair hanging down, waiting for some weak Trinidad shell cocoa that was in the sootcoated kettle to be done so that she and he could drink it with the oatmeal water for milk after the Friday herrings they had eaten at two a penny, with an egg apiece for Maggy, Boody and Katey, the cat meanwhile under the mangle devouring a mess of eggshells and charred fish heads and bones on a square of brown paper in accordance with the third precept of the church to fast and abstain on the days commanded, it being quarter tense or, if not, ember days or something like that.

It is the unconcern in his son's first reply as much as this stark image of poverty that further consigns Simon Dedalus to the shadows. But, once more, the shadows waver when Simon Dedalus's voice comes into Bloom's mind as he and Stephen walk to Eccles Street where Bloom lives. Bloom remembers Simon singing the aria from *Martha* earlier in the day, or the day before as it now is. It was, he lets Stephen know, 'sung to perfection, a study of the number, in fact, which made all the others take a back seat'. Thus his father's guilt will be tempered for a second by the memory of his father's glory.

In the final episode in the book, known as Molly Bloom's soliloquy, when Molly mentions living in Ontario Terrace, where John Stanislaus Joyce and his wife first lived after they were married, it is as though she and her husband have all along, throughout the book, been pursuing Stephen, whose mother has died, whose father had been cast aside, to become shadow versions of what his parents might have been, Bloom having taken on some of John Stanislaus's preferences such as his relishing 'the inner organs of beasts and fowls', and some of his characteristics, such as his interest in reading magazines like *Tid-bits*, as Stephen, in turn, becomes a shadow version of the Blooms' son, Rudy, who died as a baby, just as Stephen's older brother John Augustine, the first boy in the family, born in Ontario Terrace, had died as a baby.

In the soliloquy, Simon Dedalus moves from shadow to substance once more as he is remembered by Molly, remembered singing a duet with her:

> Simon Dedalus too he was always turning up half screwed singing the second verse first the old love is the new was one of his so sweetly sang the maiden on the hawthorn bough he was always on for flirtyfying too when I sang Maritana with him at Freddy Mayers private opera he had a delicious glorious voice Phoebe dearest goodbye *sweet*heart he always sang it not like Bartell dArcy sweet *tart* goodbye of course he had the gift of the voice so there was no art in it all over you like a warm showerbath O Maritana wildwood flower we sang splendidly though it was a bit too high for my register even transposed and he was married at the time to May Goulding but then hed say or do something to knock the good out of it hes a widower now I wonder what sort is his son he says hes an author and going to be a university professor of Italian . . .

*

John Stanislaus Joyce was living in lodgings with the Medcalf family in Claude Road in Drumcondra, where the best English is spoken, when *Ulysses* came out in 1922. As James Joyce became increasingly famous, he continued to treasure the family portraits his father had given him and wished to add to them by having a portrait of his father made by the Irish painter Patrick J. Tuohy, which he hung in his apartment in Paris. (Before it left Dublin, the painting was mistitled a portrait of Simon Joyce, thus merging the two fathers, one from the books, one from life.) Even Stanislaus appreciated the likeness, calling it a 'wonderful study of the old Milesian . . . The likeness is striking.' When, in turn, John Stanislaus Joyce was shown Brâncuşi's abstract image of his son James, which came in the form of a set of straight lines and spirals, he remarked: 'Jim has changed quite a bit since I have last seen him.' The old dry wit travelled with him everywhere he went.

In his book *Being Geniuses Together*, written with Kay Boyle, the American writer Robert McAlmon remembered a visit to Dublin in 1925:

In Paris, Joyce had introduced me to Patrick Tuohy, a portrait painter [who] had done portraits of Joyce and Joyce's father, and he was now conducting an art class in Dublin. While I was there he took me to see Mr. Joyce, Sr., and an amazing old man he was. He sat up in bed and looked Tuohy and me over with fiery eyes, and complained of his weakness. The fact was that he didn't like to exert himself too much, but he rang the bell, and his landlady brought barley water, and the three of us sat ourselves down to a bottle of Dublin whiskey which we had brought. He assured me that he was fond of his son James but the boy was mad entirely; but he couldn't help admiring the lad for the way he'd written of Dublin as it was, and many a chuckle it gave him. I have never seen a more intense face than that of old man Joyce.

The old man was staying in a typical boarding house of the type I had known in New York in other years. The landlady was a none too cleanly good-natured and rather shiftless Irishwoman, who complained about the trouble and work the old man caused her. But she appeared to like his presence in the house, and boasting of her own self-sacrificing nature. Before I left, Mr. Joyce had become for me the street-corner politician and aged man about town as revealed in *Ulysses*.

Just as it is strange to imagine John B. Yeats in his boarding house in New York receiving the books his son was publishing as though they were being sent to the dead – *The Green Helmet*, *Responsibilities*, *The Wild Swans at Coole*, *Michael Robartes and the Dancer* – so, too, the thought is strange of John Stanislaus Joyce in his boarding house in Dublin getting his copy of *Ulysses* in 1922, and in 1929, around the time of his eightieth birthday, being sent the de luxe edition of *Tales Told of Shem and Shaun*. It evokes the image from *Finnegans Wake* of a 'dweller in the downandouter-most where voice only of the dead may come, because ye left from me, because ye laughed on me, because, O me lonly son, ye are forgetting me!'

But John Stanislaus Joyce's son forgot nothing. And nothing was resolved by his staying away from Dublin. His father remained raw and present. Because Joyce found the space between what he knew about John Stanislaus and what he felt about him so haunting and captivating, he forged a style that was capable of evoking its shivering ambiguities, combining the need to be generous with the need to be true to what it had been like in all its variety and fullness, and indeed its pain and misery.

That style, in all its achievement, did not settle anything, how-ever, or stop Joyce from accusing himself, as though he were the one who had caused all the damage. Shortly after his father died, James Joyce's only grandson was born. The child was given the name Stephen. On the day of his birth Joyce wrote his poem 'Ecce Puer':

> Of the dark past
> A child is born;
> With joy and grief
> My heart is torn.

Calm in his cradle
The living lies.
May love and mercy
Unclose his eyes!

Young life is breathed
On the glass;
The world that was not
Comes to pass.

A child is sleeping:
An old man gone.
O, father forsaken,
Forgive your son!

# Bibliography

*The author used the following editions in his research for* Mad, Bad,
Dangerous to Know

Beckett, Samuel, *Murphy* (London, 2011)
Boland, Eavan, *A Journey with Two Maps: Becoming a Woman Poet*
(New York, 2012)
Craig, Maurice, *Dublin 1660–1860* (London, 1952)
Cronin, Anthony, *Collected Poems* (Dublin, 2004)
Cruise O'Brien, Conor, *Maria Cross* (London, 1963)
de Vere White, Terence, *The Road of Excess* (Dublin, 1945)
de Vere White, Terence, *The Parents of Oscar Wilde* (London, 1967)
Dickson, David, *Dublin: The Making of a Capital City* (Harvard, 2014)
Dudley, Anthony, *Oscar in the Wilds* (London, 2003)
Ellmann, Richard, *Oscar Wilde* (London, 1988)
Ellmann, Richard, *Four Dubliners* (London, 1988)
Ellmann, Richard, *Yeats: The Man and the Masks* (London, 2013)
Ellmann, Richard (ed.), *Selected Letters of James Joyce* (London, 2003)
Ellmann, Richard, *James Joyce* (Oxford, 1983)
Figgis, Darrell, *A Chronicle of Jail* (Dublin, 2010)
Foster, R. F., *Modern Ireland* (London, 1990)
Foster, Roy, *The Apprentice Mage* (Oxford, 1998)
Foster, Roy, *The Arch-Poet* (Oxford, 2003)
Hanberry, Gerard, *More Lives Than One* (Cork, 2011)
Holland, Merlin (ed.), *The Complete Letters of Oscar Wilde* (London, 2000)
Holland, Merlin (ed.), *Oscar Wilde: A Life in Letters* (London 2009)
Joyce, James, *Ulysses* (London, 1986)
Joyce, James, *Finnegans Wake* (London, 1999)
Joyce, James, *Stephen Hero* (London, 1963)
Joyce, James, *A Portrait of the Artist as a Young Man* (London, 2003)

*Bibliography*

Joyce, James, *Dubliners* (London, 1993)

Joyce, Stanislaus, *My Brother's Keeper* (London, 2003)

Joyce, Stanislaus, *The Dublin Diary of Stanislaus Joyce* (Cornell, 1971)

Kelly, John (ed.), *The Collected Letters of W. B. Yeats* (London and Oxford, 1986)

Kinsella, Thomas, *Collected Poems* (North Carolina, 2006)

McAlmon, Robert, and Boyle, Kay, *Being Geniuses Together* (New York, 1984)

Melville, Joy, *Mother of Oscar* (London, 1994)

Murphy, William M., *Family Secrets* (Syracuse, 1995)

Murphy, William M., *Prodigal Father* (Syracuse, 2001)

Murphy, William, *Political Imprisonment and the Irish, 1912–1921* (Oxford, 2016)

Murray, Douglas, *Bosie* (London, 2000)

O hÉithir, Breandán, and O hÉithir, Ruairi (eds), *An Aran Reader* (Dublin, 1991)

O'Sullivan, Emer, *The Fall of the House of Wilde* (London, 2016)

Robinson, Tim, *Stones of Aran* (Dublin, 1985)

Wade, Allan (ed.), *The Letters of W. B. Yeats* (London, 1954)

Wilde, Oscar, *De Profundis and Other Prison Writing*, ed. Tóibín, Colm (London 2013)

Wilde, William, *The Narrative of a Voyage to Madeira, Tenerife and along the shores of the Mediterranean* (Dublin, 1840)

Wilde, William, *The Beauties of the Boyne* (Dublin, 1849)

Wilde, William, *Lough Corrib, Its Shores and Islands* (Dublin, 1867)

Wilde, William, *Memoir of Gabriel Berenger* (Dublin, 1880)

Wilson, T. G., *Victorian Doctor* (London, 1946)

Wyndham, Horace, *Speranza* (London, 1951)

Wyse Jackson, John, and Costello, Peter, *John Stanislaus Joyce* (New York, 1998)

Yeats, J. B., Letters of *John Butler Yeats* (London, 1999)

Yeats, W. B., *Collected Poems* (London, 2003)

Yeats, W. B., *The Autobiography of W. B. Yeats* (London, 1958)

# Acknowledgements

I am grateful to Professor Ron Schuchard and Professor Geraldine Higgins at Emory for the invitation to give the Richard Ellmann Lectures and to them and their colleagues for all their kindness and hospitality.

The lectures were also published in the *London Review of Books*, and I am grateful to Daniel Soar for his skillful editorial work.

Also, I wish to acknowledge Patrick Bower for his careful and painstaking work on the contemporary reports of the Wilde/Travers case.

I wish also to thank Catriona Crowe, Ed Mulhall, Seona MacReamoinn, my agent Peter Straus, Mary Mount at Penguin UK, Nan Graham at Scribner in the US and, as usual, Angela Rohan.

# Index